Fodor's
New EDITION

Amsterdam

Reprinted from *Fodor's Holland*

FODOR'S TRAVEL PUBLICATIONS, INC.
New York and London

ISBN 0–679–02007–1

Fodor's Amsterdam

Editor: Andrew Beresky
Area Editor: Ann Campbell-Lord
Drawings: Elizabeth Haines
Maps: Jeremy Ford, Bryan Woodfield
Cover Photograph: Zeplin/Masterfile

Cover Design: Vignelli Associates

Special Sales

MANUFACTURED IN THE UNITED STATES OF AMERICA
10 9 8 7 6 5 4 3 2 1

CONTENTS

FOREWORD

Amsterdam has much to offer. It is a city fully adapted to the changing demands of a modern world, whose inhabitants have yet succeeded in evolving a dignified and preeminently intelligent way of life, in which friendship and hospitality play a major part. It is a city with a varied and eventful history, a veritable treasure house of ancient and picturesque buildings, unmistakable proof of the great cultural energy of its people, their many museums filled with countless beautiful works. It is also a city sensitively attuned to the requirements of modern tourism, placing a high priority on making life easy for the visitor—hotel and restaurant discounts, travel passes, museum deals, and the like, abound—yet still preserving that particular quality, hard to define but impossible to miss, that makes Amsterdam a special city.

* * *

Our editorial burdens have been greatly lightened by the kind support of the Netherlands Board of Tourism offices, both in Holland and London, as well as by the various provincial VVVs throughout the country. We would also like to thank Lisa Gerrard-Sharp for her efforts on our behalf.

* * *

While every care has been taken to assure the accuracy of the information in this guide, the passage of time will always bring change, and consequently the publisher cannot accept responsibility for errors that may occur.

All prices and opening times quoted in this guide are based on information available to us at press time. Hours and admission fees may change, however, and the prudent traveler will avoid inconvenience by calling ahead.

Fodor's wants to hear about your travel experiences, both pleasant and unpleasant. When a hotel or restaurant fails to live up to its billing, let us know and we will investigate the complaint and revise our entries where the facts warrant it.

Send your letters to the editors of Fodor's Travel Publications, 201 East 50th Street, New York, NY 10022.

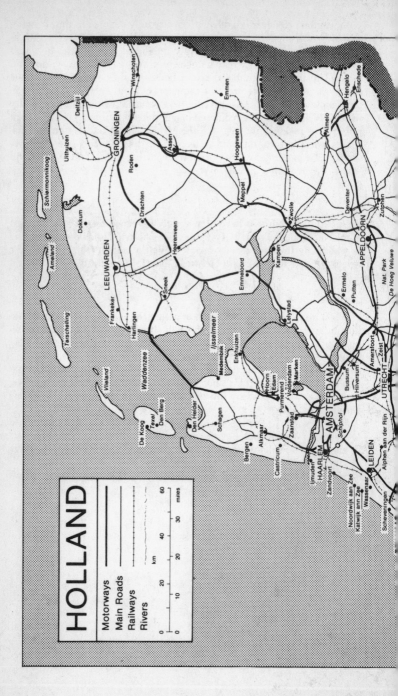

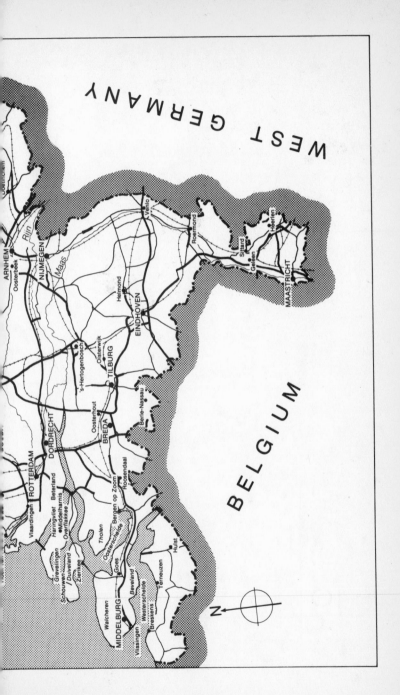

FACTS AT YOUR FINGERTIPS

Planning Your Trip

SOURCES OF INFORMATION. In this book you will find most of the information needed to plan and organize a trip to Amsterdam. However, if you do require further or more specialized information, contact the Netherlands Board of Tourism (NBT). They can supply information on all aspects of travel to and around the country, from which type of vacation is best suited to your needs and purse, to special interest and recreational travel facilities. They produce copious amounts of information, much of it free and all of it useful.

Their addresses are:

In the U.S.: 355 Lexington Ave., 21st Floor, New York, NY 10017 (tel. 212–370–7367, fax 212–370–9507); 225 N. Michigan Ave., Suite 326, Chicago, IL 60601 (tel. 312–819–0300, fax 312–819–1740); 90 New Montgomery St., Suite 305, San Francisco, CA 94105 (tel. 415–543–6772, fax 415–495–4925).

In Canada: 25 Adelaide St. East, Suite 710, Toronto, Ontario M5C 1Y2 (tel. 416–363–1577, fax 416–363–1470).

In the U.K.: 25–28 Buckingham Gate, London SW1E 6LD (tel. 071–630–0451, fax 71–828–7941).

Once in Amsterdam, you can contact the main tourist information office. Tourist offices in Holland are known as VVV.

WHEN TO GO. The main tourist season in Holland runs from about mid-April to mid-October, the peaks coming at Easter and in June to August. The weather will be at its best during this period and the country's many attractions at their most inviting during the long summer days. The Dutch, themselves, take their holidays in July and August.

However, perhaps the ideal time to visit Holland is during April and May, the height of the bulb season. Short of an unusually early spring, the bulb fields will still be colorful and some even in their prime until the end of May. Be warned, however, that at Easter hotels and other amenities are full to bursting.

Climate. Summers can be excellent, but beware sudden rains and cold winds, particularly by the sea. Winters on the other hand tend to be dull and wet, though there are a fair number of clear bright days.

Average afternoon temperatures in Amsterdam are:

	Jan.	Feb.	Mar.	Apr.	May	June	July	Aug.	Sept.	Oct.	Nov.	Dec.
°F	41	41	46	52	60	65	69	68	64	56	46	41
°C	5	5	8	11	16	18	21	20	18	13	8	5

National Holidays. National holidays are New Year's Day, Good Friday, Easter Monday, Queen's Day (April 30—shops will be open unless it's a Sunday), Liberation Day (May 5), Ascension Day, Whit Monday, Christmas (December 24–26).

PASSPORTS. Americans. Major post offices throughout the country are now authorized to process passport applications; check with your local post office for the nearest one. You may also apply in person at U.S. Passport Agency offices in various cities; addresses and phone numbers are available under governmental listings in the white or blue pages of local telephone directories. Applications are also accepted at most County Courthouses. Renewals can be handled by mail (form DSP-82) provided that your previous passport is not more than 12 years old. In addition to the completed application form (DSP-11), new applicants will need:

1. A birth certificate or certified copy thereof or other proof of citizenship;
2. Two identical photographs 2 inches square, full face, black and white or color, on nonglossy paper, and taken within the past six months;
3. $35 for the passport itself, plus a $7 processing fee if you are applying in person (no processing fee when renewing your passport by mail). For those under 18 the cost is $20 for the passport, plus a $7 processing fee— again, with no extra fee when applying by mail;
4. Proof of identity that includes a photo and signature, such as a driver's license, employment ID card, previous passport, governmental ID card. Social Security and credit cards are *not* acceptable.

Adult passports are valid for ten years, others only for five (and are not renewable). You should allow a month to six weeks for your application to be processed, but in an emergency, Passport Agency offices can have a passport readied within 24–48 hours, and even the postal authorities can indicate "Rush" when necessary.

If you expect to travel extensively, request a 48- or 96-page passport rather than the usual 24-page one. There is no extra charge. Record your passport's number and date and place of issue in a separate, secure place. When you have pictures taken for passports, have extra copies made, especially if you plan to travel extensively. You'll need photos for your International Driver's License. The loss of a valid passport should be reported immediately to the local police and to the Passport Office, Dept. of State, 1425 K Street, NW, Washington, DC 20524; if your passport is lost or stolen while abroad, report it immediately to the local authorities and apply for a replacement at the nearest U.S. Embassy or consular office.

Britons. Apply for passports on special forms obtainable from your travel agency or from the main post office in your town. The application should be sent to the Passport Office in your area (as indicated on the guidance form) or taken personally to your nearest main post office. It is advisable to apply for your passport 4–5 weeks before it is required, although in some cases it will be issued sooner. The regional Passport Offices are located in London, Liverpool, Peterborough, Glasgow and Newport. The application must be countersigned by your bank manager, or by a solicitor, barrister, doctor, clergyman or Justice of the Peace who knows you personally. You will need two photos. The fee is £15. A larger, 94-page passport can be obtained for an extra charge.

British Visitor's Passport. This simplified form of passport has advantages for the once-in-a-while tourist. Valid for one year and not renewable, it costs £7.50. Application may be made at a local post office (in Northern Ireland at the Passport Office in Belfast); you will need identification plus two passport photographs—no other formalities.

Canadians. Canadian citizens may obtain application forms for passports at any post office; these are to be sent to the Bureau of Passports, External Affairs, Ottawa, Ontario K1A 0G3,with a remittance of $25, two photographs, a guarantor, and evidence of Canadian citizenship. You may apply in person to the regional passport offices in Edmonton, Halifax, Montreal, Toronto, Fredericton, Hamilton, London, Ottawa, Hull, Quebec, St. John's, Saskatoon, North York, Victoria, Windsor, Vancouver or Winnipeg. Canadian passports are valid for five years.

Visas. Visitors to Holland from the U.S., Canada, the U.K., Australia and New Zealand, plus most European and Commonwealth countries, do not require visas to enter Holland for stays of up to three months. South African visitors will need a visa.

Health Certificates. These are not required from any country.

TAKING MONEY ABROAD. Traveler's checks are still the standard and best way to safeguard your travel funds; and you will usually get a better exchange rate in Europe for traveler's checks than for cash. Your choice of branch will depend on several factors. American Express checks are widely known, Bank of America has some 28,000 correspondents throughout the world, Thomas Cook about 20,000. The best-known British checks are Cook's and those of Barclays, Lloyds, Midland and National Westminster banks.

Major credit cards are accepted in most large hotels, restaurants and shops but most do not accept all cards, so check at each place in advance. Out of major cities, credit cards are not so widely accepted. It is possible to obtain cash from banks for most leading international credit cards, usually for a minimum of Fl. 400, but a service charge, sometimes rather high, will be made. A passport will be needed for identification.

Europeans holding a Uniform Eurocheque card and check book—apply for them at your bank—can cash checks for varying amounts at banks participating in the scheme, and can also write checks for goods and services—hotels, restaurants, shops.

We give details in the section Dutch Currency.

HEALTH AND INSURANCE. Travel insurance can cover everything from health and accident costs, to lost baggage and trip cancellation. Sometimes they can all be obtained with one blanket policy; other times they overlap with existing coverage you might have for health and/or home; still other times it is best to buy policies that are tailored to specific needs. But, insurance is available from many sources and many travelers unwittingly end up with redundant coverage. Before purchasing separate travel insurance of any kind, be sure to check your regular policies carefully.

Generally, it is best to take care of your insurance needs *before* embarking on your trip. You'll pay more for less coverage—and have less chance to read the fine print—if you wait until the last minute. Best of all, if you have a regular insurance agent, he is the person to consult first. Flight insurance, often included in the price of the ticket when the fare is paid via American Express, Visa or certain other major credit cards, is also often included in package policies providing accident coverage as well. These policies are available from most tour operators and insurance companies. While it is a good idea to have health and accident insurance, be careful not to spend money to duplicate coverage you may already have . . . or to neglect some eventuality which could end up costing a small fortune. For example, Blue Cross-Blue Shield policies cover health costs incurred while traveling. They will not, however, cover the cost of many types of emergency transportation, which can often add up to several thousand dollars. Emergency transportation *is* covered, in part at least, by many major medical policies such as those underwritten by Prudential and Metropolitan. Again, check any policy carefully before buying. Note that most insurance issued specifically for travel does not cover pre-existing medical conditions.

Several organizations offer coverage designed to supplement existing health insurance and to help defray costs not covered by many standard policies, such as emergency transportation. Some of the more prominent are:

Carefree Travel Insurance, c/o ARM Coverage Inc., 120 Mineola Blvd., Box 310, Mineola, NY 11501, underwritten by the Hartford Accident and Indemnity Co., offers a comprehensive benefits package that includes trip cancellation and interruption, medical, legal, and economic assistance. Trip cancellation and interruption insurance can be purchased separately. Call 800–343–3553 for additional information.

International SOS Assistance Inc., Box 11568, Philadelphia, PA, 19116, has fees from $25 a person for up to fourteen days, to $195 for a year (tel. 800–523–8930).

IAMAT (International Association for Medical Assistance to Travelers), 417 Center St., Lewiston, NY 14092 in the U.S. (tel. 716–754–4883); or 40 Regal Road, Guelph, Ontario N1K 1B5 (tel. 519–836–0102).

Travel Assistance International, the American arm of *Europ Assistance,* offers a comprehensive program providing medical and personal emergency services and offering immediate, on-the-spot medical, personal and financial help. Trip protection ranges from $40 for an individual for up to eight days to $600 for an entire family for a year. Full details from travel agents or insurance brokers, or from Europ Assistance Worldwide Services, Inc., 1133 15th St., N.W., Washington, DC 20005 (800–821–2828). In the U.K., contact Europ Assistance Ltd., 252 High St., Croydon, Surrey CRO 1NF (081–680 1234).

The Association of British Insurers, Aldermary House, Queen St., London EC4N 1TT (tel. 071–248 4477), will give comprehensive advice on all aspects of vacation travel insurance from the U.K. Send a self-addressed envelope for the *Holiday Insurance* brochure, which lists procedures and registered members.

Loss of baggage is another frequent inconvenience to travelers. It is possible, though complicated, to insure your luggage against loss through theft or negligence. Insurance companies are reluctant to sell such coverage alone, however, since it is often a losing proposition for them. Instead, this type of coverage is usually included as part of a package that also covers accidents or health. Should you lose your luggage or some other personal possession, it is essential to report it to the local police immediately. Without documentation of such a report, your insurance company might be very stingy. Also, before buying baggage insurance, check your homeowner's policy. Some such policies offer "off-premises theft" coverage, including the loss of luggage while traveling.

Trip cancellation coverage is especially important to travelers on APEX or charter flights. Should you be unable to continue your trip during your vacation, you may be stuck having to buy a new one-way fare home, plus paying for the charter you're not using. You can guard against this with "trip cancellation insurance." Most of these policies will also cover last-minute cancellations.

STUDENT AND YOUTH TRAVEL. Perhaps the single most important aid to youth travel throughout Europe is the International Student Identity Card, which is generally needed to get special youth or student discounts in—travel, theater, museum passes, etc. Similarly, you must have a card to get the excellent Eurail Youth Pass. Within Holland the most important address for contact and information is the Netherlands Youth Hostel Center, Prof. Tulpplein 4, 1018 GX Amsterdam (tel. 020–551–3155).

The ISI Card can be obtained at all of the General Student Travel Service Organizations. You can also get it from the Council on International Educational Exchange, 205 East 42 St., New York, NY 10017. Canadian students should apply to the *Canadian Federation of Students-Services,* 187 College St., Toronto, Ontario M5T 1P7. It is generally easier and cheaper to get all special membership cards and passes *before* you leave home, for example, membership in your national youth hostel association, international student card, student rail pass, International Driving Permit, etc.

HINTS FOR DISABLED TRAVELERS. Facilities in Holland for disabled visitors are generally good. The Netherlands Board of Tourism produces an informative free brochure, *Hotel and Recreation Opportunities for the Disabled,* which lists many hotels, restaurants, museums, places of interest, etc., with facilities for disabled visitors.

Otherwise, the major sources of information are: *Access to the World: A Travel Guide for the Handicapped,* by Louise Weiss, available from Henry Holt & Co., Box 30135, Salt Lake City, Utah 84130 (tel. 800/247–3912); the *International Air Transport Association,* 2000 Peel St., Montreal, Quebec H3A 2R4, for their pamphlet *Incapacitated Passenger's Air Travel Guide;* the lists of commercial tour operators who arrange travel for the disabled published by the Society for the Advancement of Travel for the Handicapped, (SATH), 26 Court St., Penthouse Suite, Brooklyn, NY 11242; and the Travel Information Service at Moss Rehabilitation Hospital, 12th St. and Tabor Rd., Philadelphia, PA 19141.

The main source for information in Britain for all advice on disabled travel is The Royal Association for Disability and Rehabilitation (Radar), 25 Mortimer St., London W1N 8AB (tel: 071–637 5400). Another possibility is Mobility International, 228 Borough High St., London SE1 1JX (tel. 071–403 5688). Mobility International Holland's contact address in Holland is Postbus 165, 6560 AD Groesbeek (tel. 08891–97111).

LANGUAGE. Dutch is a relatively impenetrable language to most English speakers, but except in the most out of the way places (and sometimes not even then) you are unlikely to have any difficulties. English is widely spoken in all major tourist centers—hotels, restaurants, rail stations etc.— while at all tourist offices there will always be at least one fluent English speaker, though the odds are there will be more. Indeed, you are liable to find that even bus conductors and street cleaners speak pretty good English. But nonetheless, if you can manage a few words or phrases in Dutch, it will be appreciated. It is polite to say *Dag!* (Good day) when entering and leaving a shop. In restaurants, you'll be wished *Eet smakelijk!* (Enjoy your meal). See our *English-Dutch Vocabulary* for useful words and phrases.

DUTCH TIME. Holland is on Central European Time, six hours ahead of the East Coast of the United States, nine hours ahead of the West Coast. It is one hour ahead of the U.K.

Staying in Amsterdam

CUSTOMS ON ARRIVAL. There are two levels of duty-free allowance for visitors to Holland. For travelers arriving from a non-EC country the allowances are:

200 cigarettes or 50 cigars or 250 grams of tobacco; plus one liter of spirits more than 22% proof or two liters of spirits less than 22% proof or two liters of liqueur wine or two liters of sparkling wine, plus two liters of wine; plus 50 grams of perfume and 250 ml. of toilet water; plus other goods to the value of Fl. 125.

For travelers arriving from an EC country, the allowances for goods, provided they were *not* bought in a duty-free shop, are: 300 cigarettes or 75 cigars or 400 grams of tobacco; plus one and a half liters of spirits more than 22% proof or three liters of spirits less than 22% proof or three liters of sparkling wine or three liters of liqueur wine, plus five liters of non sparkling wine; plus 75 grams of perfume and 38 centiliters of toilet water; plus other goods to the value of Fl. 910.

All personal items may be imported duty free, provided you take them out with you when you leave. Tobacco and alcohol allowances are for those 17 and over. There are no restrictions on the import and export of Dutch currency.

DUTCH CURRENCY. The monetary unit in Holland is the *gulden* (guilder or florin), written as Fl. Notes are in denominations of 1,000, 250, 100, 50, 25, and 10 guilders. Coins are 5 and 2.5 guilders, 1 guilder, 25, 10, and 5 cents. Be careful not to mix up the 2.5 guilder and the 1 guilder coins as there is not much difference in size. Bank notes have a code of dots that can be identified; this is for the blind.

At the time of writing (mid-1990), the exchange rate for guilder was Fl. 1.70 to the U.S. dollar and Fl. 3.25 to the pound sterling. However, these rates change constantly, so check them carefully while planning your trip and during it.

Changing Money. Changing money is easy in Holland. You can do so either at banks (open 9–4 or 5, depending on the branch, Mon.–Fri.) or through the many GWK bureaux de change offices. These are located in main stations, airports, key border crossings and in a number of major tourist centers. They offer good rates and are open Monday through Saturday 8–8 and on Sunday 10–4. GWK offices in Amsterdam Central Station, in major cities, and on border crossings are now open 24 hours per day. Hotels and some shops will also change major foreign currencies, but usually at less than favorable rates. GWK will also accept major credit cards to obtain cash. Thomas Cook and some other commercial organizations now operate exchange offices in Amsterdam, but banks generally give the best exchange rates.

HOTELS. Dutch hotels are generally excellently-run, spotlessly clean and extremely comfortable. Holland offers a wide range of accommodations, from luxurious international hotels to country inns, farmhouses and traditional small town hotels.

Don't be surprised if your waiter hands you your room bill after you finish breakfast and are preparing to leave. This is typical of smaller establishments and is in fact really quite convenient as it eliminates further delay at the time of your actual departure.

It is usually possible to make reservations either by writing or calling hotels, but there is an excellent reservations system operated by the Netherlands Reservations Center; this service is free. Contact Netherlands Reservations Center, Vlietweg 15, 2260 AK Leidschendam (tel. 070–320–2500). Alternatively, some VVV offices operate accommodations services for a small fee, but bookings need to be made in person. We give addresses for VVV offices in the *Practical Information* section.

YOUTH HOSTELS. Ask the NBT for its brochures entitled *Holland, a Young and Lively Country* and *Group Accommodation*. Holland has over 50 youth hostels, mostly providing very clean dormitory style accommodations but very few other facilities. In order to use them, you must be a member of the International Youth Hostels Federation. Bed and breakfast costs around Fl. 20–35 a night. Hostels in cities tend to get very full in the summer, particularly in Amsterdam. Full lists of all youth hostels may be had from the Netherlands Youth Hostel Center (LJHC), 4 Prof. Tulpplein, 1018 GX Amsterdam (tel. 020–551–3133) or from any branch of the NBT or VVV.

BED-AND-BREAKFASTS. These are found all over Holland and are very popular. Most are family-run and very inexpensive. There is no overall national listing of bed and breakfast places, but many VVV offices have local lists. However, they can get very full in high summer. Prices for a double room range from Fl. 25 to Fl. 30 per person, including breakfast. The NBT's *Bed and Breakfast* brochure lists VVV offices and the number of beds available in the area.

RESTAURANTS. The complex and rewarding subject of eating in Holland is covered in our Dutch Food and Drink chapter. However, a number of general points should nonetheless be noted.

First remember that the Dutch like to eat early—normally around six or seven in the evening. Even in many expensive restaurants, the kitchen tends to be closed by 9 or 10. Most, however, only accept last orders earlier than this. In larger towns, some "foreign" restaurants stay open until midnight. Most, especially the better ones, can also get very full, so it is nearly always strongly recommended to book ahead. Credit cards are generally, but not universally, accepted—always check if yours will be or you could find yourself in a very embarrassing situation. Note also that more expensive restaurants usually have dishes in more than one price category, so that what appears an expensive restaurant can sometimes prove quite reasonable if you choose carefully. All Dutch restaurants are legally obliged to display their menus in the window; study them carefully and you could find yourself a bargain. Keep your eyes open, too, for the excellent-value Tourist Menu. This costs around Fl. 20 (by law) and must have three courses. All restaurants serving them have a sign in the window. The *Nederlands Dis* red, white, and blue soup-tureen sign is a promise of regional recipes and seasonal ingredients at moderate prices (a three-course dinner for two for under Fl. 120). At the opposite end of the spectrum, the *Alliance Gastronomique Néderlandaise* group of restaurants offer Dutch-French gourmet cuisine (at gourmet prices). For special occasions, the *Romantische Restaurants* are appropriately set in romantic locations such as castles, stately homes, or old inns. Prices are Moderate-Expensive. Ask the NBT or VVV for brochures on *Tourist Menus, Nederlands Dis, Alliance Gastronomique,* and *Romantische Restaurants.*

TIPPING. All hotels and restaurants in Holland include 15% service and value added tax. It is usual to give small extra gratuities for special help or service. Give the doorman, for example, Fl. 1 for calling a cab. It is also customary to leave any odd small change when paying a bill.

Hairdressers and barbers have inclusive service prices, but they do expect a tip of at least 10%. Taxis in almost every town have a tip included in the meter charge, but here again the fare is made up to the nearest guilder by the user. Where the tip is not included, add the odd 50 cents.

The official minimum for railway porters is Fl. 2.50 a bag. Ushers at cinemas, theaters and concerts are usually given 25 cents for showing you to your seat although this is not necessary. Hat-check attendants expect at least 50 cents, but more according to the type of place. Washroom attendants get Fl. 1 as a general rule.

TELEPHONES. The telephone system in Holland is excellent and thoroughly reliable. All towns and cities have area codes which you must use if you are calling from outside that area. (We give the Amsterdam area code in the Practical Information section that follows). Long distance and international calls are easily made; country codes are given in telephone directories. If you wish to make a call via the international operator, all of whom speak English, dial 06–0410, but this service is not available through coin-operated booths. For overseas directory service (information), dial 06–0418, or 06–022–9111 for an AT&T operator.

Be sure to read the instructions if you are calling from a public phone booth as there are a number of different types. Low rates are charged between 7 P.M. and 10 A.M. and from 7 P.M. on Fridays to 10 A.M. Mondays. Always have plenty of coins available for long distance calls. Local calls cost 25 cents or 50 cents, depending on the site of the call. The average cost per minute to the U.S. is Fl. 2.60. To dial yourself: dial the international code 09 first, wait for a second tone then dial the country code (1 for the U.S.), followed by the area code (less the initial 0, or 9 for Spain and Finland) then the personal number.

However, whatever you do, avoid making calls, especially long distance calls, from your hotel room. Hotels regard telephone calls as a secret source of revenue and sometimes charge as much as three times the actual cost.

MAIL. The Dutch post office is as efficient as the telephone service, thanks in part to the modest size of the country and the concentration of population.

Airmail letter rates, to Europe up to 20 gr., 75 cents, to U.S.A. and Canada up to 10 gr., Fl. 1.30. Postcards, to Europe 55 cents, to U.S.A. and Canada 75 cents. Aerogrammes, 60 cents to Europe, Fl. 1 to U.S.A. and Canada. (Increases to these prices are expected.)

CLOSING TIMES. Shops are open weekdays from 8.30 or 9 till 5.30 or 6. Some are also open from 7–9 P.M. on Thursdays or Fridays. Many of the smaller neighborhood shops close during the lunch hour from 1–2. All shops are compelled by law to close one half-day each week; this may be during the morning or afternoon, and varies from shop to shop. Most department stores and many shops are closed Monday mornings, while some restaurants close one evening a week, usually Mondays or Tuesdays. There is late-night shopping on Thursday in Amsterdam. Banks are open from 9 to 4 or 5 Monday through Friday, closed Saturdays.

Be sure to double check all opening times of museums and galleries on the spot. Hours and closing days are not standardized and we have found that such times are liable to be changed with no notice at all, due to staff shortages, strikes, fire and Acts of God, and you could make a trip only to find a locked door.

ELECTRICITY. The standard in Holland is 220-volt, 50-cycle alternating current. So most American appliances will need transformers to convert them to 220-volt operation. Some hotels have only 120V, while others have wall-plugs allowing for either 220 or 120V. Dutch wall outlets (mains) require a larger plug than the kind used in the United States.

BABY-SITTERS. These can be obtained through students' organizations, especially for the evenings. Rates are from Fl. 5 to Fl. 10 an hour until midnight and up to Fl. 15 afterwards. Check with your hotel, or the local VVV office for details.

GUIDES. There is an official organization for guides in the Netherlands: GUIDOR, Box 3351, 1001 AD Amsterdam (tel. 020–624–6072). Guides can be hired by the hour. They are qualified and multi-lingual. Alternatively, many VVV offices can advise on knowledgeable people to show you around.

SECURITY. As in many countries throughout the world, Holland is now plagued by an influx of petty thievery. Particularly in Amsterdam and its environs are visitors advised to take precautions. Whenever you can, leave your valuables in your hotel room or safe. Don't leave bags or purses unattended, especially at buffet-style restaurants or cafeterias, which have become favorite spots for petty thieves.

Leaving Amsterdam

CUSTOMS ON RETURNING HOME. If you propose to take on your holiday any *foreign-made* articles, such as cameras, binoculars, expensive timepieces and the like, it is wise to put with your travel documents the receipt from the retailer or some other evidence that the item was bought in your home country. If you bought the article on a previous holiday abroad and have already paid duty on it, carry with you the receipt for this. Otherwise, on returning home, you may be charged duty (for British residents, Value Added Tax as well). In other words, unless you can prove prior possession, foreign-made articles are dutiable *each time* they enter the U.S. The details below are correct as we go to press. It would be wise to check in case of change. In Holland, purchases of over Fl. 300 made in one store qualify for a Sales Tax Rebate (VAT refund) of 18.5%. This can be claimed at the airport but you need to have asked the salesperson for the appropriate form.

U.S. Residents may bring in $400 worth of foreign merchandise as gifts or for personal use without having to pay duty, provided they have been out of the country more than 48 hours and provided they have not claimed a similar exemption within the previous 30 days. Every member of a family is entitled to the same exemption, regardless of age, and the exemptions can be pooled. For the next $1,000 worth of goods a flat 10% rate is assessed.

The $400 figure is based on the fair retail value of the goods in the country where acquired. Included for travelers over the age of 21 are one liter of alcohol, 100 cigars (non-Cuban) and 200 cigarettes. Any amount in excess of those limits will be taxed at the port of entry, and may additionally be taxed in the traveler's home state. Only one bottle of perfume trademarked in the U.S. may be brought in. Write to the U.S. Customs Service, 1301 Constitution Ave., Washington, DC 20044, for information regarding importation of automobiles and/or motorcycles. You may not bring home meats, fruits, plants, soil or other agricultural items.

Gifts valued at under $50 may be mailed to friends or relatives at home, but not more than one per day (of receipt) to any one addressee. These gifts must not include perfumes costing more than $5, tobacco or liquor.

Military personnel returning from abroad should check with the nearest American Embassy for special regulations pertaining to them.

Canadian Residents. In addition to personal effects, and over and above the basic exemption of $300 a year, the following articles may be brought in duty free: a maximum of 50 cigars, 200 cigarettes, 2.2 pounds of tobacco and 40 ounces of liquor, provided these are declared in writing to customs on arrival and accompany the traveler in hand or checked-through baggage. Personal gifts should be mailed as "Unsolicited Gift—Value Under $40." Canadian customs regulations are strictly enforced; you are recommended to check what your allowances are and to make sure you have kept receipts for whatever you have bought abroad. For details ask for the Canada Customs brochure, "I Declare."

British Residents. There are two levels of duty free allowance for people entering the U.K.; one, for goods bought outside the EC or for goods bought in a duty free shop within the EC; two, for goods bought in an EC country but not in a duty free shop. The Netherlands is a member of the EC.

In the first category you may import duty free: 200 cigarettes or 100 cigarillos or 50 cigars or 250 grammes of tobacco (*Note* if you live outside Europe, these allowances are doubled); plus one liter of alcoholic drinks over 22% vol. (38.8% proof) or two liters of alcoholic drinks not over 22% vol. or fortified or sparkling wine; plus two liters of still table wine; plus 60 milliliters of perfume; plus 250 milliliters of toilet water; plus other goods to the value of £32.

In the second category you may import duty free: 300 cigarettes or 150 cigarillos or 75 cigars or 400 grammes of tobacco; plus 1½ liters of alcoholic drinks over 22% vol. (38.8% proof) or three liters of alcoholic drinks not over 22% vol. or fortified or sparkling wine; plus five liters of still table wine; plus 90 milliliters of perfume; plus 375 milliliters of toilet water; plus other goods to the value of £250. (*Note* though it is not classified as an alcoholic drink by EC countries for Customs' purposes and is thus considered part of the "other goods" allowance, you may not import more than 50 liters of beer). Tulip bulbs are best packed and transported by a specialist firm. Try Wijs Royal Bulb Export, Singel 508, by Amsterdam's floating flower market.

In addition, no animals or pets of any kind may be brought into the U.K. The penalties for doing so are severe and are strictly enforced; there are *no* exceptions. Similarly, fresh meats, plants and vegetables, controlled drugs and firearms and ammunition may not be brought into the U.K. There are no restrictions on the import or export of British and foreign currencies.

DUTCH ARTS, CRAFTS
AND LETTERS

Merchants and Old Masters

Dutch art speaks with many voices, and is sometimes blithely silent—as though smugly aware that tradition, in the long haul, will overtake the periods that turn out daubs and make do. To find a beginning to the tradition (traditions would hit it off just as well), one could go back just as far as one felt like and begin to make out one's plausible case. One could begin with the Romans' brief hegemony over the land that was to become the Netherlands. Next might come the relics, in the southeast of this territory, of Byzantine influence, when the Middle Ages were young and unlabelled. One could do worse than say that before the 14th century there was no Dutch art. Instead, there were a number of foreign influences working away at the fashioning of a native art. There were Germanic elements, and, in the 14th century, came French elements.

Claus Sluter, who was born in Haarlem about the middle of the 14th century, was the most important sculptor of his time. But at an early age he moved to Dijon, in France, to work for the dukes of Burgundy, so when his Dutch talent developed, it was outside Holland. At Dijon he fashioned great tombs testifying to the grandeur of the dead nobility. He has been called the first of the modern sculptors, and his realism, his plastic expressionism, and his individual treatment of figures influenced the art of sculpture in Europe until the end of the 15th century.

The greatest painters at this time, when the dukes of Burgundy ruled the lands that were one day to become known as Holland and Belgium, were undoubtedly Hubert and Jan van Eyck. Born at Maaseik, near Maastricht, in the second half of the 14th century, the two brothers did not represent a sudden and unexpected upsurge of painting. Although they are regarded as the founders of the Flemish School, their work, heralding the beginning of the Renaissance in the north, was the result of a long and integrated line of capable artists, but their genius eclipsed their precursors. Hubert's life is an almost complete mystery. Jan, his junior by 19 years, was first employed by John of Bavaria, and was then engaged by Burgundy's Duke Philip the Good. He worked in Bruges, mightily developing the art of portraiture. As a favorite of the Duke he also went on a pilgrimage and several secret missions. In 1428 he accompanied an Embassy to Portugal where he painted two portraits of the Infanta Isabella as well as taking part in negotiations on behalf of Philip, who was suing for her hand.

The style developed by his Flemish School, so finely represented in its early stages by Albert van Ouwater (1400-80) and his pupil Geertgen tot Sint Jans (1465-93), has become known as "primitive." As in Italy, the northern quattrocento looked back into its own past, and used what it found there to produce new ideals. In Italy the model was antiquity. In the Netherlands, where an energetic bourgeoisie looked out toward a wider world, the Gothic style lent its ancient idiom to the new art. This is why northern Gothic seems to have lasted for so long. But the outer shell was animated by a new and vigorous force.

But there was another fundamental difference between the development of the Italian and Northern Renaissances, a difference that was particularly pronounced in the Low Countries and that was to exert an enormous influence on Dutch arts. In Italy, and to some extent France as well, patronage of the arts was the almost exclusive preserve of the Church and the ruling families. Painting, sculpture and architecture were accordingly either courtly and aristocratic in character or religious. In the Low Countries on the other hand, especially after the Reformation and into the 17th century, patronage was principally in the hands of a powerful and influential merchant class. The necessary consequence of this was that the arts were predominantly bourgeois in character; that is, portraiture, especially group portraits, landscapes and views, and flower painting—all basically forms concerned with the real world as opposed to the largely idealized world of Italian paintings—were most common. And of course the existence of this wealthy merchant class, able and willing to patronize the arts, was, in addition to shaping the character of Dutch arts, crucially important to its continued existence and development, the primary precondition of all sustained artistic endeavour being the means to practise it.

From Bosch to Hals

However, at the end of the 15th century, Dutch art was still fundamentally medieval in character, as the nightmare visions of Hieronymus Bosch (c. 1450–1516) make very clear—the rational and lucid paintings of the 16th century were still very much a development for the future. Bosch is a compelling painter, strangely in tune with modern tastes. His complex religious allegories, which have provoked comparisons with Surrealism—a notion that the painter himself would be at a complete loss to understand—present an endlessly fascinating and detailed vision of late medieval concerns. Unfortunately the exact meaning of much of his haunted work is not known, but his success may be judged from the fact that many of his best pictures belonged to Philip II (and are accordingly now housed in the Prado in Madrid).

Among other leading figures of this period was Cornelis Engelbrechtsz (1468–1533), founder of the Leiden School of painting. One of his most important pupils was Lucas van Leyden, the leading figure of the artistic transition from the Gothic to the Renaissance during the early years of the 16th century. Where Engelbrechtsz seemed limited by formal conceptions, Lucas van Leyden inclined towards the freer Italian style. His great portraits did much to forward the trend towards secularizing art. When he died in 1533, aged 37, he was ranked with Dürer and Marc Antonio Raimondo as one of the greatest etchers of his time.

Half a century after Bosch, Pieter Brueghel the Elder (1529-69), who lived during the tumultuous times of the Spanish wars, brought a deep understanding of the tragedy of destruction, poverty, and illness to his robust and realistic canvases. And it was in the latter part of the 16th century that the most characteristic forms of Dutch painting developed. The period as a whole witnessed the development of Holland's great portraiture; at the same time came a wholesale, religious-inspired destruction of much of the great Catholic art which had been building up through the generations. Into the 17th century, the peculiarly Dutch tradition of group portraiture gradually evolved. Civil groups and professional societies were soon having large group portraits of themselves painted. The century also saw the quick growth of a number of tendencies: there were artists who grew great at the art of suggesting rather than laying bare on canvas. The Dutch were witnessing the full bloom of the work which earned their artists the title of "painters of the bourgeoisie". Comparatively little of Dutch art before the 17th century—except portraits—has survived. The inspiration of Calvin had led to the destruction of stained-glass windows, church statues, and canvases.

Frans Hals (1580-1666) has been called the first modern painter. He succeeded in transfixing on canvas the outward appearance of the bourgeoisie. A fantastically adept and naturally gifted man, he could turn out a portrait in an hour. He delighted in capturing the emotions of a moment—a smile or a grimace—in an early manifestation of the same impressionist preferences that were to capture art in the 19th century. He spent most of his life in Haarlem (where much of his work can be seen in the authentic 17th-century building of the Frans Hals Museum), and he has perhaps justly been called the founder of the Dutch School—a term encompassing the supreme art that flourished for a century.

Rembrandt and the Stirring 17th Century

Rembrandt van Rijn (1606–69), born a quarter-century after Hals, was the greatest of the Dutch School—therefore, perhaps, the greatest Dutch artist of all time. Born in Leiden, the fifth child of a miller, he grew rich from painting and tuition paid by his pupils; for a while his wealth was such that he became a noted collector of art. Into his first works he painted a heap of over-ornamentation, but then, as the years went by, he dug deeper and deeper into the essence of his subjects and portrayed the incessant metaphysical struggle for inner beauty and reason. When his whole material world crashed about him, though he was blackmailed and ruined, he unaccountably continued to turn out art that grew greater and greater. His marvelously skilled use of light and shadow is a text and source of wonder for living artists. A master of landscapes, still-lifes, and Biblical scenes as well as portraiture, his greatness as a painter has tended to eclipse his glory as an etcher and draftsman. In the graphic arts he was the last example of the "Renaissance man." His most imposing work, *The Night Watch,* can be seen at Amsterdam's Rijksmuseum. Some of his finest self-portraits hang in the Mauritshuis at Den Haag.

Holland's political golden era came during the second half of the 17th century, and though the art of the day was pale compared to Rembrandt's, it is nonetheless great. With only one million people in the Netherlands, there was nevertheless a superabundance of great masters. Jan van Goyen began fashioning the neglected art of landscape painting (which previous artists had usually been interested in merely as background). So, then, did Albert Cuyp and Jacob van Ruysdael. Jan Vermeer (1632–75) was born in Delft and died in Delft, and for all any historian knows never left the town. There are about 40 paintings ascribed to him. Vermeer brought genre art to its peak; in small canvases of a sometimes overwhelming realism, he painted the soft calm and everyday sameness of scenes from middle-class life, with the subjects caught and held fast in the net of their normal surroundings. His *View of Delft,* in the Maritshuis Museum in Den Haag, is considered the greatest of all Dutch town portraits.

Pieter de Hoogh (1629–85) painted pictures that have been called architectural; i.e., the people seem to have been introduced to heighten interest in the buildings and only after the buildings have been painted in. Jan Steen, who was born in Leiden in 1626, painted occasionally great, sometimes biting or humorously satiric canvases, full of human bustle and animation. He was the painter *par excellence* of the Dutch shopkeeper and his family—the lower middle class. He had trouble finding a market for his art; when he died he is supposed to have had on hand 500 unsold canvases. Gerard Terborch (1617–81) developed a mastery at painting textile texture, and served up a series of thoughtful conversation pieces, posing his subjects talking. He also developed tremendous skill at miniature-scale, full-length portraits. The son of a tax collector, he appears to have done a good deal of traveling and to have painted only in his spare time.

With their strong maritime interests it is not surprising that Dutch marine painters were among the most important painters of their time. The first notable artist in the field was Hendrik Vroom (1566–1640) who worked mainly in his native Haarlem. Simon de Vlieger (1600–53) is known for his peaceful sea themes and as the teacher of two other respected marine artists of the period, Jan van de Capelle (1624–79) and Ludolf Bakhuizen (1631–1708).

Perhaps the best known and admired of all were the van de Veldes, Elder and Younger. Willem van de Velde the Elder (1611–93) was present in a semi-official capacity at a number of the sea battles between the Dutch and British and recorded what he saw with superb depth and craftsmanship. His son, also Willem, (1633–1707) also painted sea battles and, like his father, spent his later years in England, under the patronage of Charles II.

Dutch marine artists, like their colleagues on land, were interested in recording the reality of their subjects, and they did so with consummate skill and style. They developed this particular school of painting to a level of mastery seldom challenged elsewhere and their works are prominently hung in a number of leading galleries.

At the end of the 17th century a decline set in that was characterized mainly by a lack of vigor and individuality and a preoccupation with color and gaudy ornamentation. In the 18th century interest was directed more towards the decorative arts, such as painted panels, ceilings and wallpaper, and the exterior ornamentation of the home.

The 19th and 20th Centuries

Around the middle of the 19th century a new trend became noticeable, the best-known interpreter thereof being J. B. Jongkind. This rebirth of Dutch art, The Hague School, as it became known, with painters like Joseph Israels and Jacob Maris, coincided with the French Impressionists. A representative collection of its work (as well as of the Barbizon School) can be seen in Den Haag at the Rijksmuseum H. W. Mesdag, housed in the former home of H. W. Mesdag (1831–1915), who also painted the interesting Mesdag Panorama.

Vincent van Gogh (1853–90), an individualist, the servant of no school, but the unwitting master of many a painter, left Holland to bring his private revolution in art to southern France. But Holland now honors him with a wide-ranging selection of his works in many museums, notably Amsterdam's Rijksmuseum Vincent Van Gogh and the Rijksmuseum Kröller-Müller near Otterlo.

Towards the end of the 19th century Breitner and Isaac Israels founded the Amsterdam Impressionists, followed during the early years of the present century by Jan Toorop and Johan Thorn Prikker, representing the Art Nouveau movement. The Bergen School (called after the resort town of Bergen near Alkmaar), led for a time by the Frenchman Le-Fauconnier, who lived in Holland during World War I, carried on the renewed tradition of vigor and individuality. Hendrik Chabot painted rough-looking peasant figures which closely resemble the work of today's Flemish master, Constant Permeke. Other painters belonging to this school are Kees van Dongen, Jan Sluyters, Leo Gestel, and Piet Mondriaan, whose work during this early period clearly indicates the beginning of Dutch Fauvism. *De Stijl* (Style), a movement that took its name from the magazine published by an *avant garde* post-World War I group, blew simplicity into the cluttered structure of art (and architecture), notably with the work of Piet Mondriaan, Theo van Doesburg, and Bart van der Leck. Van Doesburg and Mondriaan drew canvases made up of rectangles of white and primary colors separated by thick or thin black lines. The period between the two world wars was dominated by two trends, the expressionism of painters like Charley Toorop, Hendrik Chabot, and Charles Eyck, and a form of neo-realism represented by Raoul Hynckes and A. C. Willink.

After World War II the New European School was represented in Holland by the Informal Group. Amongst the best-known modern Dutch painters are Kees van Dongen, Jaap Wagemaker, Willem de Kooning, Sierk Schröder, Karel Appel, Carel Willink, Gerrit Benner, Co Westerik, Bram van der Velde, Corneille, G. Veenhuizen, and Jan van Heel. In more recent years, a small group of painters and sculptors established *Fugare* in Den Haag, a movement whose main purpose is to counterbalance the lack of aim or form they feel is apparent in too much of the work of the younger generation of artists.

In the field of graphic art Holland has a long and rich tradition. The most strikingly original among recent graphic artists was Maurits Escher who died in the early 1970s.

Stained Glass and Sculpture

During the 16th century Holland produced some outstandingly fine stained glass, of which only a small amount survived the Reformation. The best examples, made by the brothers Dirck and Wouter Crabeth, can be seen in the St. Janskerk in Gouda. Although the following centuries saw a large production of attractive work, and the art is still practiced fairly extensively today, it never again achieved the same standard of greatness.

Except for Rombout Verhulst (1624–98), the Dutch have had no sculptor since Claus Sluter they could call of a truly great international character. During the 20th century, however, there has been a tentative resurgence of attempts at creative sculpture, but the current work is hardly inspired. Henry Moore, Zadkine, Arp and Marini have exerted a profound influence. Among the most successful modern sculptors are Professor V. P. S. Esser, Wessel Couzijn, Hildo Krop, Lottie van der Gaag, and the Japanese-born Tajiri. The greatest modern sculptor is perhaps Mari Andriessen (1897–1979) who created the powerful sculpture *The Docker* that stands beside Amsterdam's Portuguese Synagogue.

Great Galleries

Among the abundance of public and private art collections in the Netherlands, the two greatest are Amsterdam's Rijksmuseum and Den Haag's Mauritshuis. The former, if not quite in the same class as the Louvre or the Prado in terms of size, still must be ranked among the top half dozen in Europe for quality. It is strongest in the Dutch masters of the 16th and 17th centuries, of course, but is by no means limited to them or even to painting alone. Its collection of prints and etchings is possibly the finest in the world.

The small and intimate Mauritshuis in Den Haag fills the visitor with unabashed delight. This gracious 17th-century former palace houses a collection that boasts only first-class work. Housed in magnificently restored surroundings, its quality is great enough to warrant a lifetime of study.

After these two rank the Stedelijk Museum at Amsterdam and the Gemeentemuseum (Municipal Museum) at Den Haag, both emphasizing 19th and 20th-century Dutch art. The former is especially noteworthy for its extensive modern collection, the latter for Dutch painting since the 17th century. Rotterdam's museum Boymans-van Beuningen is housed in a delightful modern building, and its collection of paintings is well worth a visit.

A very valuable addition in 1973 was the opening of the Vincent van Gogh Museum near the Stedelijk Museum in Amsterdam. This contains one of the world's richest collections of works of art of one period, in the form of paintings, drawings and letters by Vincent van Gogh placed on permanent loan to the Netherlands State. The artist's full collection of prints and many sketches form part of the treasure, which comprises altogether about 200 paintings and 400 drawings by van Gogh as well as works by his contemporaries like Gauguin, Bernard and Monticelli. In addition to being a unique exhibition, it also serves as a research center, with a library, extensive archives and a studio/workshop, available to specialists, students and painters.

Among other specialized museums are Haarlem's Frans Halsmuseum, the previously mentioned Rijksmuseum H. W. Mesdag at Den Haag (with one of the finest collections of Impressionist works outside France), and the Rijksmuseum Kröller-Müller near Otterlo (north of Arnhem in central Holland), which includes a fine collection of van Goghs.

Collections, or part-collections, are sometimes loaned to other museums at home or abroad, so if there are certain exhibits you particularly want to see remember to check beforehand or you may be disappointed. Remember that the *Museumkaart* entitles you to free admission to most nationally operated Dutch museums.

Progressive Architecture

Romanesque influences can be detected in the architecture of some of the older towns, especially in the southern provinces. The Pieterskerk in Utrecht is the best example of the Romanesque in the Netherlands. During the Gothic period, when other nations were building gigantic cathedrals, Holland built smaller ones. The marshy ground makes great and heavy buildings impractical, which accounts for the fact that most of the churches have wooden, instead of stone, vaults.

The Renaissance, when it came to Dutch architecture, was fairly conservative, but only by comparison with the effects it brought in other countries. The baroque, in Dutch architecture, was never to be given free rein. Instead there was developed a form of restrained classicism, the best examples of which are the Mauritshuis and the façade of the Houses of Parliament facing the Vijverberg in Den Haag, and the Royal Palace in Amsterdam.

For a long time, Dutch architects were content to imitate foreign styles, re-creating them in "neo" forms. But there was always that prime necessity to think in terms of the given elements: the marshy ground, the available building materials. Whole towns were built on piles sunk into the swampland. The Royal Palace in Amsterdam, for example, built during the first half of the 17th century, is supported by some 13,600 piles.

It is, perhaps, in the field of domestic architecture that the Dutch have made their most important contribution to the face of Europe. The town houses lining the canals of cities like Amsterdam have much individuality in design and character yet, over all, create an outstanding sense of aesthetic cohesion. In England, much of the riches created by imperial and commercial expansion were poured into great country houses, but in Holland, particularly during the 17th century, wealthy merchants in spices and other trade from the Indies, built on a much smaller scale. Their homes were compact, outwardly relatively restrained and often served as offices and even warehouses for their owners, as well as homes. But there is no denying their taste, nor the obvious wealth they represented. Old Dutch houses, as in so many manifestations of the Dutch character, reflect the nature of the people: conservative, cautious about wasting space or money, but not above wanting to demonstrate to outsiders how successful they were!

The visitor to any of the older Dutch cities should look carefully at these ordinary houses, they are one of the most delightful and enjoyable aspects of sightseeing.

Another of the most delightful sights on Holland's architectural scene are the *hofjes, begijnhofs,* or almshouses. These miniature residences are usually grouped around a central courtyard, and many of them can be visited.

The great Dutch architect, Hendrik Petrus Berlage (1856–1934), had by the late-19th century broken with current styles, substituting for them a rationalist style. Gradually the functionalists supplanted the traditionalists. The Amsterdam School brought the expressionist influence. *Stijl* had a profound influence on architecture, advocating as it did a simplicity and economy of structure, and the doing away with excessive ornamentation. Thousands of buildings (and especially schools) bear the earmarks of the functionalists' concepts. Although in the past building had been based on brick construction, during this century more and more concrete faced with granite, marble, sandstone and so forth is used. The Dutch were the first ever to use glass bricks as structural elements. In buildings everywhere, more and more thought was given to bringing sunlight into the home. Windows grew broader and broader, and now the great expanse of glass in homes and offices is one of the most superficially striking features of the cityscape. World War II, sadly enough, proved a tremendous stimulant to that same architecture, for with wide destruction came the need for extensive rebuilding: in the Netherlands, urban planning is a major profession. Today's Dutch architecture is characterized by a sense of order and conciseness. Color is another striking feature—everywhere patently visible, if not always underdone. Not long ago, 10-story buildings were considered to be skyscrapers in Holland, and there were not many of those. Now blocks of flats with 20 stories or more are popping up faster than tulips in springtime. Modern Dutch architecture is succeeding in achieving considerable variety and attractiveness of design for both industrial buildings and new housing, with Rotterdam in the lead. In Rotterdam, *Lijnbaan,* created in 1952–4, was the first pedestrian shopping arcade in Europe. Urban sprawl has eaten into the landscape—Amsterdam, Den Haag, Rotterdam and Dordrecht are separated only by short stretches of open fields. As a natural reaction, the present trend is to create more 'natural' architectural environments with buildings set in landscaped gardens, if possible near water. Within a decade these cities are expected to have been merged, absorbing the little towns and villages in between, to form one long city along the coast which is known as *Randstad Holland* (Rim-City Holland).

Arts and Crafts

In the decorative arts, as in the fine arts, Holland's artisans and craftsmen first borrowed and copied heavily from foreign teachers. Dutch pottery, for example, was strongly influenced by Spanish and Italian decoration and form. In the beginning of the 17th century Holland evolved a national pottery of its own—the famed blue and white Delftware—though this was, indeed, inspired by Chinese porcelain. The greatest potters were soon centered in Delft, which now produces the well-known Delft blue.

However, a new generation of artist-potters has appeared, started by Christiaan J. Lanooy, continued by Lambertus Nienhuis, and greatly fostered by the well-known Delftware makers De Porceleyne Fles. The firm is one of only two genuine Delftware makers in the city. A great deal of talent emerged from that firm's experimental studio and some lovely ceramics are now being made by artists who have abandoned both tradition and ostentation.

In the manufacture of glassware, foreign sources again provided initial impetus, followed once more by a gradual shift to greater austerity, which finally fashioned itself into a Dutch style. Dutch domestic glass—decanters, wineglasses etc.—reached a high order of design and execution from the 16th century onwards. Basic shapes tended to be simple and solid, but the superb etching and engraving skills of Dutch craftsmen turned them into works of art, which can still be seen and enjoyed in various museum collections of domestic glass throughout Holland. The best modern Dutch crystal comes from Leerdam, and the finest of the Leerdam products are usually the simplest, the most regular, the most blankly austere in design.

Tiles—a third, well-known product of Dutch artisanry—were best made in and about Rotterdam. At first the tiles were used in Dutch floors only, but their popularity and practicality were such that it soon became common practice for whole walls to be covered with tiles, in the Arabic manner.

The Dutch have always loved silver. It represented a solid and portable form of wealth which could demonstrate not only the affluence, but the taste of the owner. As early as the mid-16th century Dutch silversmiths, influenced by designs from Germany (especially Nuremberg and Augsburg), France and Spain, began to produce fine work for the guilds, churches and domestic patrons. Influenced by Gothic forms, but tending towards much heavier pieces than seen in, say, France, Dutch craftsmen evolved their own distinct character and techniques. Utrecht became a major center for silversmiths after the Seven Provinces united in 1579 and, during the 17th century, the craft flourished in other cities, particularly Amsterdam, Haarlem, Leiden and Dordrecht. Today, however, the best place to see silversmiths creating original designs is Schoonhoven, an easy drive from any of the major cities in the Randstad.

The elaborate Dutch version of Baroque style in the mid-17th century dominated European taste, and Dutch craftsmen perfected techniques for engraving on silver never surpassed elsewhere. Dutch silversmiths also favored the use of heavy embossing and high relief, particularly in dishes and plaques. The rich guilds commissioned massive commemorative works and private families often recorded births and marriages with specially engraved pieces. In church plate the influence of the Reformation produced more restrained designs than was generally seen in domestic silver, but overall the quality of Dutch craftmanship was outstanding. It is a tragedy that the constant international and civil wars which racked the country caused much of this magnificent work to be lost, melted down to pay for various military needs, but enough remains in museums in Holland to show how superb was the Dutch control over this rich medium.

Dutch Literature

Dutch literature is one of the anomalies of the country's culture. Since authors, as a rule, write in their native language, Dutch authors are doomed to a limited readership that can be expanded only through translation. There has always been a shortage of skilled translators for Dutch literature. But the Dutch themselves, subjected to a schooltime regime that includes heavy, compulsory doses of French, English, and German, take pride in reading foreign literature in the original language. Perhaps the greatest influences on Dutch literature have come from outside Holland's borders—from the foreign authors whose works Dutch authors came to know so well.

Thomas à Kempis (1380–1471), the German author of the *Imitatio Christi,* made Holland his home and died in a monastery near Zwolle. Desiderius Erasmus (1467–1536), sometimes called the Dutch Voltaire, sometimes The Prince of the Humanists, was born in Rotterdam. In the 16th century, the artistic center of gravity moved from the south (present-day Belgium) to the north, notably Amsterdam. Grotius, who lived in the 16th and 17th centuries, wrote the first great texts on international law, especially those concerning the conduct of war. The philosopher Descartes, though a Frenchman, lived in Holland for 20 years, extolling the cool climate, claiming it helped him think more clearly.

Baruch Spinoza (1632–77), one of the philosophy greats of all time, was born in Holland of Portuguese parents who had fled the Inquisition in their home country. He was educated in Holland, lived by working as a grinder of lenses, and developed a pantheistic philosophy that scandalized the Jewish community's theological leaders. Spinoza's first great work—*Tractatus Theologico-Politicus*—published anonymously, pleaded for religious freedom and higher (i.e. scientific) criticism of the Bible.

Perhaps as a reaction to strait-laced morality and narrow-mindedness, Dutch literature is at its greatest in the lyric form. The very strictness of moral injunction has been cast in a soaring form of lyric expression. The greatest Dutch poet was Joost van den Vondel (1587–1679). Vondel wrote classic, often baroque, Alexandrine verse tragedies in five acts, treating subjects of occasional great remoteness and loftiness. Thirteen of his tragedies had Biblical subjects. He was the son of a couple from Antwerp who took refuge from the Inquisition in Cologne, then moved to Amsterdam. From the age of ten, Vondel lived there; for a time he was an accountant at the municipal pawn shop. Partly because of poetry's translation difficulties, Vondel is hardly known outside Holland.

The Dutch statesman and poet Jacob Cats (1577–1660), known affectionately as 'Father Cats', wrote poetry about ordinary, devout people in a form easily remembered and quoted. P. C. Hooft (1581–1647) was one of the most urbane of poets, who gathered about him, in his castle at Muiden, a group of artists, musicians, and authors. Constantijn Huygens, father of the physicist Christiaan, was yet another of the gifted Dutch versifiers, the fashioner of a spare style which nevertheless managed to bulge with pithiness. Gerbrand Adriaanszoon Bredero was that strangest of all classic Dutch literateurs: a thorough Bohemian.

As in painting, Holland's native literature suffered a long period of something less than greatness during the 20th century. During World War

Il some great poetry was written by an occasional resistance worker, and in the 1960's and 1970's a young generation of Dutch poets sprang up which attracted attention mainly because they broke all the normal rules of poetry and produced extraordinary stream-of-consciousness works.

Though Dutch literature is seldom translated, and its market rarely goes farther than Dutch-speaking Flanders, in Belgium, Dutch authors produce a startling number of works. Three-fourths of Dutch books are first editions. Some of Holland's youngest authors have taken the bull by the horns and now write in English in order to reach a wider public. Among the better-known Dutch authors abroad are Jan de Hartog, Johan Fabricius, Hans Martin, Willy van Hemert, Willem Frederick Hermans, Pieter de Vries, Gerard Reve, and van Eysselstein. Equally well known are Simon Carmiggelt and Godfried Bomans, both of whom died in recent years. A separate Frisian literature has existed since the 17th century and, despite its limited circulation, continues to flourish.

Music and the Theater

Although such composers as Jacob Obrecht (1455–1505), Jan Sweelinck (1562–1621), Alphonse Diepenbrock (1862–1921), and Willem Pijper (1894–1947) had considerable influence upon their contemporaries, rare is the Dutchman who will do much bragging about his country's record in composing music. This attitude is not wholly justified. Research in recent years has led to the rediscovery of a host of minor composers whose work had been relegated to oblivion.

In performing music, however, the Dutch do not bow their heads to anyone. Amsterdam's Royal Concertgebouw Orchestra, which celebrated its centenary in 1988, was led towards European supremacy by Willem Kees, and under the late Willem Mengelberg was believed to have reached the pinnacle of its fame. However, it is continuing to improve its deserved reputation. The Hague Philharmonic (Residentie) Orchestra is Holland's second-best, and there are a number of cities and towns, such as Rotterdam and Utrecht, boasting orchestras of their own. The Dutch also have their own National Opera Company which gets a great reception all over Europe for the standard of its performances and the imagination behind its productions. Stolid though the Dutch may seem to be, they love music. There are choral societies, chamber music groups, and village bands and fanfares beyond number. In the smaller towns as well as in the larger cities recitals on ancient church organs and famous carillons can be heard regularly.

Nor do the Dutch limit their musical tastes. Every Dutchman will tell you that to hear Bach's St. Matthew Passion performed in the 15th-century church at Naarden at Easter is a unique experience no music-lover should miss, but he will also extol the rollicking tunes churned out by one of the many gaily baroque barrel organs that roam the streets in fair weather. And contrary to what one might have expected, the Dutch, with the Belgians, are the best exponents of jazz and swing in Europe. To name but a very few of the best performers: the beautiful and sophisticated pianist and singer Pia Beck, Pim Jacobs' Jazz Trio with the brilliant vocalists Rita Reys, Soesja Citroen, and the Dutch Swing College Band, the Dixieland Pipers, and a number of pop groups which have won European renown.

There are also many music contests and festivals held all over Holland. At Kerkrade, in the southeast of Holland on the German border, a World Music Festival is held every four years, the next in the summer of 1994. Den Haag is the home of the annual North Sea Jazz Festival, an international event that regularly attracts major stars from abroad.

Perhaps the biggest event is the Holland Festival, which takes place annually during June. Although some programs are presented throughout the country, and a few specialized features take place only in one or other of the smaller towns, the majority of performances are held in and around Amsterdam. Performances of Dutch music, drama and dance are alternated with the best other countries can offer in the field of new theatrical productions, contemporary music and choreography. Although most of the guest programs are provided by neighboring countries, some come from as far afield as Peru or India. The Holland Festival has won generous acclaim from the international press and is now ranked with the renowned Salzburg and Edinburgh festivals.

Faced with the difficulties of a severely limited audience at home and little chance of touring abroad because of the language barrier, the Dutch theater has no chance of counting on a large and profitable run of a single play. Its survival, therefore, depends largely on government subsidies. There is a good deal of traveling by theater companies within Holland and the repertoires are usually large. There is a growing coterie of Dutch playwrights, although there is still a tendency to produce translated performances of foreign plays and musicals. The Dutch do, however, excel in revues, cabaret or *kleinkunst* ("small art" forms). A special mention should be made of the Nederland Dance Theater ballet company which many consider to be among the most important of modern contemporary groups in Europe.

The Dutch are not particularly renowned for their contribution to the cinema, though their efforts in this medium have gained more international attention in the past ten years. Most of the films that are shown are imported and screened in their original language, with Dutch subtitles. The contemporary arts scene, particularly in Amsterdam, is one of the liveliest in Europe. Much credit is due to the government's generous subsidies to artists, and to the catholic tastes of the younger generation. The Dutch are enthusiastic museum-goers and attach great value to well-designed exhibitions.

FOLKLORE AND TRADITIONAL EVENTS

Rich Panorama of Customs and Costumes

As could be expected of a nation with so rich a past and with such veneration of tradition, the Dutch are steeped in their special folklore and folkways. Their tradition, bearing the marks of their history and of their religion, displays itself in their work and in their play, in their dress and in their habits.

We will not subject you here to any deep study of ethnology. But we will try to cover, discursively and impressionistically, enough of the Dutch folklore so that you may understand a little better the strange things you see as you travel through the country. For those more interested in the national ways and habits, we would suggest a visit to the Het Nederlands Openluchtmuseum (Netherlands National Open-Air Museum) at Arnhem, where you can see, spread over acre after acre, samples of Dutch houses, costumes, and rural life, exhibited in a manner that will help you to understand the differences between one region and another.

It is neither true—as you may have gathered from movies and musical comedies—that all Dutch people disport themselves in quaint costumes and wooden shoes, nor—as you may suspect after visiting some of the places where costumes are worn—that they are a sham, invented and perpetuated to gull the guileless tourist. What is true is that at one time regional costumes were prevalent in many parts of the country, that they have almost died out under the impact of modern influences. Occasionally, they can still be seen in those relatively isolated areas where there is resistance to the machine age.

You will not see traditional lace caps, golden earrings, and billowing skirts in big towns. But there are areas where costumes—mainly worn by women, but also by men in some cases—are the daily dress, the living representation of an ancient heritage. For those interested in costume-hunting, the best grounds are the shores of the IJsselmeer (the former Zuiderzee), the fishing harbor at Den Haag's seaside resort of Schevening-en, the islands of Zeeland, and, to a certain extent, the rural areas of eastern and southern Holland.

If costumes are of more than passing interest to you, then you must not miss the Zuiderzee Museum at Enkhuizen, 33 miles northwest of Amsterdam. An entire floor of this fascinating museum, housed in a building that once belonged to the East India Company, has been given over to sample interiors of homes and demonstrations of crafts that are typical of the Zuiderzee region. Each of the authentically furnished rooms is livened by the presence of dummy figures dressed in the local garb. Although the collection is not complete—it does not include areas beyond the Zuiderzee—it is nonetheless fascinating and worthwhile.

Where Regional Costumes Are Still Worn

Best publicized, of course, are the twin towns of Volendam and Marken, a scant dozen miles north of Amsterdam, where costume-wearing and the selling of souvenirs to tourists have become the main sources of livelihood. You can even dress up yourself and have your picture taken, provided you can fight your way through the bus loads of other tourists. Go if you must, but remember that the clothes are the only authentic feature of this commercially orientated parade.

In Volendam, the women wear a blue-striped or black-pleated skirt and a jacket. Young girls wear a bonnet with a high point. The costume is completed by a colorful apron, patent slippers, and a red-coral necklace. The men sport exaggeratedly baggy trousers and, on Sundays, a fascinating jacket, closely fitted at the waist and decorated with a massive silver button and chain.

Over at Marken, a former fishing village sitting high and dry following the completion of yet another Zuider Zee polder, the women wear a long-sleeved shirt under a sort of cotton vest (waistcoat) with red-and-white striped sleeves. On top of this rather masculine get-up they femininely wear an embroidered bodice, a woollen yoke, a sleeveless jacket, and finally another square yoke of flowered cotton. Their headgear is a bonnet with a cardboard form to keep it in shape. The men wear baggy black (or sometimes, in summer, white) trousers, a bright red sash, a blue smock with white collar, a neckerchief, and gold throat buttons. Girls and young boys are dressed alike in checked bibs, bonnets, and aprons. (But white bibs and blue skirts for the boys.)

When you visit Den Haag, you may notice portly ladies doing their shopping in severe black dresses whose hems practically touch the ground. They are wives of the fishermen at nearby Scheveningen, where you will see even more of these dignified matrons going about their business without the slightest trace of selfconsciousness, although the younger generation now usually prefer modern dress and, with a shrug of embarrassment, refer to the costumed women in certain regions as "black stockings." Although the sea-colored shawls, in shades of blue, green, and grey (red-lined black capes in winter) enliven the somber skirts, your eye will most likely be attracted to a pair of gold, horn-like ornaments that protrude from the spotless white cambric bonnets (lace on Sundays) that invariably cover their heads. These oval filigree decorations are part of a gold hair band that is concealed by the bonnet.

Something rather similar is characteristic of the islands of Zeeland in the southwestern corner of Holland, which are less frequented by visitors because of their remote location. The town of Goes is the best center, especially on Tuesday market days. There are marked differences between the dress of Protestants and Roman Catholics. Protestant women wear a bonnet shaped somewhat like a conch shell, and Catholic women a bonnet shaped like a trapezium with a light-blue under bonnet beneath. Catholic women usually wear brighter colors than the Protestants. With the bonnet go the burnished gold "ear irons". The most important element of the South Beveland costume is a yoke combined with a *beuk,* a garment covering bosom and back, often made of flowered silk. Men wear black knee-breeches and silver belt buttons. There are local variations in costume from one part of Zeeland to another.

Less far afield are the twin towns of Spakenburg and Bunschoten on the southern shore of the IJsselmeer, roughly 30 miles east of Amsterdam and near the garden-like cities of Hilversum and Amersfoort. Costumes are now rarely seen here, but when they are, Spakenburg has the more interesting of the two. Its chief features are what appear to be shoulder boards, a yoke of brightly-flowered cotton that stands out so stiffly from the neck that a slim girl looks something like a knight in armor, and a husky young lady suggests a tackle on an all-star football team. A tight-fitting cap tends to make the head look shrunken above this massive shoulder line, perhaps explaining why the husbands were formerly fishermen and stayed away for days on end.

The most charming, most genuine, and most colorful costumes are worn by the farming families that live along the road joining Rouveen and Staphorst, a few miles north of Zwolle, which lies between the IJsselmeer and the German border. Should you detour to include these delightful villages on your itinerary, remember that picture-taking is deeply resented. In the past, if you were to attempt a photo on a Sunday when the pious farmers walk to church in silent files, you would risk physical assault for invading the privacy of these otherwise cheerful villagers; so be sure to ask first.

As for the Staphorst costumes, the women wear bolero-like bodices with black-and-blue striped skirts whose hips have been strangely padded. A wide, deep collar with painted flower motifs is worn except when a woman is in mourning. A red checked cotton neckerchief and large silver show buckles are added on Sundays. Beneath a white lace cap lurk silver "ear irons" with golden curls. The men boast watch chains, gold buttons on a white collar, and a double row of silver buttons on the shirt. Boys and girls dress alike up to the age of three or four.

At Urk, a one-time island that now forms the southwest tip of the Noordoostpolder, about 25 miles northwest of Zwolle, women wear a partly visible corset of light blue on which chamois leather is sewn to prevent wear. The costume itself is stiffened with whalebone. The Urk men wear

baggy black trousers held together with silver belt buttons, plus black
shirts, shoes, and caps. But remember that even today no cars or even bicycles are allowed within the Urk village center on Sundays. And don't start
up your radio either within church earshot.

There is a colorful folklore procession, and traditional Dutch and West
Frisian dances are performed each Thursday during July and August in
Schagen, North Holland.

Distinctive costumes are worn in other districts and villages of Holland,
and if you are interested in knowing about more of them, detailed studies
with extensive illustrations may be bought in English editions at larger
bookstores in Amsterdam and Den Haag.

Traditional Holidays

The Dutch love food—especially sweets, pastries, and whipped cream—
so it is no wonder that many of their holidays are associated with particular delicacies. Most festivals, of course, are religious in origin, still retain-
ing a devotional atmosphere. Here are the significant ones.

December 5th—and not Christmas, as in Great Britain and the United
States—is the occasion for exchanging gifts, although this custom is also
rapidly changing. It is presided over by St. Nicholas, or Sinterklaas, as
the Dutch call him. This is in fact the origin of the name Santa Claus,
but unlike the polar Santa Claus, this one makes his entry from Spain.
He has the same white beard as Santa Claus, but he is dressed in a sweep-
ing red robe, a red and gold miter, and carries a bishop's golden crook.
He is attended by his Moorish servant, Zwarte Piet, or Black Peter. Most
Dutch families celebrate the day by meeting in the evening to place shoes
by the fireplace which during the night are filled with presents. St. Nicholas himself, however, appears on the 3rd or 4th Saturday in November.
In Amsterdam the whole city turns up to welcome him as he makes his
way from the harbor to the center of the city. He is officially welcomed
in front of the Stadhuis, the City Hall, by the Lord Mayor. St. Nicholas
then makes a speech of his own, praising or reproaching the people as he
sees fit. At the same moment, he and his helpers suddenly appear all over
the rest of the country. Six weeks before St. Nicholas Day, shops blossom
with marzipan in every shape and form, fondant, *speculaas* (spiced ginger
cookies), *taai-taai* (spiced cake) in the form of animals and figures, and
nine-inch-tall chocolate initials. Equally characteristic is the *banketletter*,
a pastry initial filled with almond paste.

Until recently Christmas itself was not a time of festivity. But almost
all over the country now it has been influenced by the Anglo-American
customs. So, in addition to still being a family affair Christmas is nowadays
little else but a prolongation of the St. Nicholas festival earlier in the
month, and in many cases, especially in families where the children have
grown up, is celebrated with much more jollification than the earlier feast.
Almost every Dutch family now has a Christmas tree, and a thriving new
industry has sprung up in the designing, producing and selling of Dutch
Christmas cards, while all department stores and stationers' shops also
sell a wide variety of cards in English. The shops, too, now treat Christmas
as a wonderful second St. Nicholas festival, both in decorations and presents.

Winter celebrations and festivities in Holland immediately suggest the fabulous winter scenes of Pieter Brueghel or Jan van Goyen, to name but two of the many Dutch 17th-century painters who have done so much to color the popular image of Christmas the world over. For some reason, winters never seem quite as snowy or picturesque in Holland these days, but the country's lakes and canals still regularly freeze over and then a series of ice-skating races, whose origins stretch back many centuries, take place. Whole towns and villages turn out to watch, with suitable feasting and drinking afterwards. The most famous is held, conditions permitting, in Friesland in February and attracts country-wide excitement (the saying goes that children here are born with skates on their feet). The race goes by or through 11 towns, hence its name: Elf-Steden-Tocht, simply, the Eleven Town Race. It covers a gruelling 200 km. (125 miles) and starts at seven in the morning, when it is still dark and decidedly cold. Many competitors are still battling their weary way around the final stretches of the course at midnight. But with typical Dutch thoroughness, check points and first aid stations line the route to help those who don't make it.

Easter, as might be expected, features the bunny and the egg, with merry hunts for buried eggs and a special Dutch game called *eiertikken* in which children bump their eggs together to see whose will be broken first. But, in addition, there are some unusual regional customs. In some places in the eastern and southern provinces, "Easter bonfires" are lit to celebrate the spring-blazes that are reminiscent of the old fertility fires. In a few rural places girls are still covered with soot—a direct vestige of another ancient fertility rite.

Among other characteristic holiday customs are *dauwtrappen* (treading the dew), the dawn trip to the country on Ascension Day; the St. John's procession during June in the woods near Laren, ending at the "Old Cemetery", the reputed site of one-time heathen sacrifices; and the Whitsun Crowns in the Frisian village of Hindeloopen, consisting of hoops decorated with fir branches, garlands, paper roses, and eggshells.

Among secular holidays, the most important are the Queen's Day on April 30th, a time when the larger cities are festooned with the royal standard and with clusters of orange-colored balls in honor of the House of Orange. Every year, the queen selects one town where she visits with the people to celebrate the day. In Den Haag, on the third Tuesday in September, Queen Beatrix opens Parliament, arriving in a golden coach amid much cheerful pomp.

Market days can be witnessed in a wide variety, depending on the region and on what is being marketed. One of the most famous is built around the cheese trade in Alkmaar, which started in 1571 as a special privilege granted by the king. The carrying and weighing are part of an ancient ritual, and you need only see the cheese-laden barrows and costumed porters to realize that this is a tradition buried in antiquity. The market runs on Fridays only, mid-April to mid-September, from 10 to midday. Almost as interesting is the Gouda cheese market on Thursday mornings from 9 to 12.30, mid-June to mid-August. You can sample the cheese in the charming old town hall and watch a color film illustrating how Gouda cheeses are made.

A number of "Folk Markets" are held throughout the year, such as that in Hoorn. From July to mid-August, the market is held every Wednesday with handicraft displays, folk dancing and local craft demonstrations. A similar market is that at Westerbroek in Drenthe. This also displays old crafts, but gives you a chance to admire the delightful old costumes of the area. A newer market is the Kaasmarkt, Cheese Market, at Purmerend. Here, porters wearing the historic uniform of the ancient Cheese Guild, solemnly weigh and carry the cheese. It takes place from 10 to 1 every Thursday, mid-June to mid-August.

Carnival in Holland does not reach the heights attained in the Latin countries, but in the more Catholic south and east there are many festive celebrations worth seeing—especially in such towns as Maastricht and 's-Hertogenbosch (Den Bosch). In recent years, Amsterdam has also jumped on the bandwagon, with a carnival parade and festivities. These celebrations are riots of costumes and merrymaking, all presided over by "Prince Carnival". The Dutch Carnival is usually held seven weeks before Easter.

In larger cities, New Year's Eve has become another very popular Dutch excuse for merrymaking. Although end-of-the-year balls are held only in the large hotels and restaurants, most Dutch wait up enjoying the special TV or radio programs so that they can participate in street fireworks displays. Amsterdam traditionally rings in the New Year with fireworks, church bells ringing, ships' sirens in the harbor, rattles, saucepan lids, in fact anything that makes a noise. Doughnuts without holes, called *oliebollen*, are usually eaten on New Year's Eve and sometimes a coin is hidden in one of them, or in a cake. Finding it is a mixed blessing as the finder has to treat everyone to cakes or other goodies.

Local Customs and Sports

The fishing ports have age-old local customs, of which the most stirring is the spring departure of the luggers and trawlers for the herring grounds. Once the sailings were filled with poignancy because of the long absence and dangers involved, and an aura of the momentous still surrounds this traditional event. For weeks in advance, herring casks are scrubbed, the boats painted and made shipshape. On sailing day the villages are gaily decorated with flags and there is much excited speculation as to who will bring back the first boatload of new herring—the first cask of which is traditionally presented to the Queen. IJmuiden, Scheveningen and Vlaardingen take turns in putting on an elaborate festive display.

Traditional sports can still be seen in the Netherlands, such as the Frisian ball game of *kaatsen,* the archery clubs, and *vendelzwaaien,* the banner-waving displays in the south. A typical traditional sport is the Walcheren *ringrijderij,* at Middelburg during August, in which men mounted on horses aim their lances at small rings. The winner receives the Queen's beaker.

DUTCH FOOD AND DRINK

Homelike or Exotic—Always Hearty

Holland can offer you a large variety of cooking, while the frequent trips which Dutch executives make abroad have served to ensure that the foreign cuisine in Holland, when it is good, is very, very good. But real Dutch cooking is made of sterner stuff. Simple, solid nourishment, without any fancy trimmings that might hide the basic high quality of the food, is what warms the cockles of the average Dutch heart. As a result, Dutch cooking is often called unimaginative. This is only relatively true. An abundant variety of meat, fish and fowl, vegetables and fruit, at reasonable prices, do not oblige the Dutch cook to resort to ingenuity when preparing a meal. The true Dutch cook is inclined to be lavish with butter and the result is often a strain on the digestive systems of those used to lighter fare.

At the other extreme, Indonesian food, with its variety of spices and exotic dishes, provides a dramatic contrast to the blander Dutch fare. But in between nowadays, almost every large town has a wide range of restaurants specializing in their own brands of 'national' dishes, running from Chinese to Italian, French to Yugoslavian, and even American to English. Most of the local tourist offices (VVV) have restaurant lists which will help you to explore the best in each area.

When to Eat

The mealtime pattern is remarkably uniform throughout Holland. Breakfast invariably consists of several varieties of bread and rolls, thin slices of Dutch cheese, prepared meats and sausage, butter and jam or honey, often a boiled egg, and a pot of steaming coffee, tea, or chocolate. Fruit juices are generally available but not cheap.

Don't be astonished if the waiter presents you with your hotel bill when you have finished breakfast (assuming you are preparing to leave). This custom, especially prevalent at provincial hotels, is actually a convenience and saves you the trouble of having to settle up at the last minute.

The typical lunch is *koffietafel,* which consists of more bread, various cold cuts, cheese and conserves. There is usually a side dish—warm (an omelette, a small individual cottage pie, or the like) or cold (a salad, Russian eggs, or something similar)—to go with it. The whole is washed down with tea or coffee.

The evening meal is usually the major repast of the day and is often eaten quite early—6 P.M. to 6.30 P.M. Outside the major cities, most kitchens close well before 10 P.M.

Coffee at 11 in the morning (or earlier) and tea at 4 in the afternoon are equally sacred rituals.

What to Eat

Tradition has its place in Dutch eating. Although many dishes which were a part of the Dutch way of life before the advent of heated greenhouses, canning, deep-freeze, and modern transport facilities are now no longer a necessity, people still relish them.

To start with soup, there are two which can be called typically Dutch. *Erwtensoep*—a thick pea soup, usually only available October through March, often served with pieces of smoked sausage, cubes of pork fat, pig's knuckle, and slices of brown or white bread. *Groentensoep*—a clear consommé, loaded with vegetables, vermicelli, and tiny meatballs.

Hutspot—a hotchpotch of potatoes, carrots and onions with a historical background. When the siege of Leiden was raised on October 3rd, 1574, the starving populace was given, first, salted herring and white bread, then *hutspot* with *klapstuk* (stewed lean beef of which a little goes a long way). This has become such a traditional dish that you will find Dutchmen eating it on October 3rd anywhere from the North Pole to the Equator, from New York to Hong Kong.

Herring—eaten all the year round, the Dutch delight in the salted variety, but especially in "green herring" (those caught during the first three weeks of the fishing season which starts in May). You can eat herring neatly filleted and served on toast as an hors d'oeuvre in any restaurant, but half the fun is buying it from a pushcart, holding the herring by the tail, and gobbling it down like a native. The first cask of new herring is traditionally presented to the Queen.

Rolpens met Rodekool—thin slices of spiced and pickled minced beef and tripe, sautéed in butter, topped with a slice of apple, and served with red cabbage.

Boerenkool met Rookworst—a hotchpotch of frost-crisped kale and potatoes, served with smoked sausage.

Zuurkool—Sauerkraut: "garni" means with streaky bacon, gammon, and sausage.

Stokvis—an old-time favorite few restaurants serve nowadays. If you'd like to try something really different this is your dish. The basis is dried whitefish, cooked in milk and drained, served with potatoes and rice, fried onions, sliced raw onions, chopped dill pickles, melted butter and mustard sauce.

Kapucijners—Marrowfat peas, served with boiled potatoes, chunky pieces of stewed beef, fried bacon cubes, french fried onions, slivers of raw onion, dill pickles, mustard pickles, melted butter, molasses, and a green salad. Believe it or not the result is delicious.

Remember that nearly all the above dishes, like so many traditional dishes in Europe, are winter fare.

Seafood—fish of all kinds is usually well prepared in Holland. Try, for example, *gebakken zeetong* (fried sole) or *lekkerbekjes*—specially prepared fried whiting. Royal imperial oysters, mainly from Zeeland, are still an epicurean dish, while the smaller equally tasty "petites" are also good. Both types, however, are expensive. Dutch shrimps are delicious, but often small. If your purse is well filled, try lobster (but ask the price first), as this is a real luxury. Crab is rarely available. Mussels, on the other hand, are cheap, and if you love them there's always a fish restaurant somewhere around, or buy them, fried in batter or pickled, from a fishmonger. Eel is another specialty. It is served either fresh or smoked and filleted, on buttered toast. It has a bouquet and flavor that is more easily praised than described; the smaller-sized eels taste better than the large ones. In this form it normally serves as an hors d'oeuvre. It is also eaten stewed or fried (but again, ask the price first).

Cheeses—These are not usually eaten at the end of the meal but play a considerable part in lunch or as snacks. Edam and Gouda are deservedly famous, whether eaten *jonge* (fresh) or *oude* (mature). Leiden cheese is often eaten with an aperitif; Frisian cheese is flavored with cloves.

Dessert—Here the Dutch, on the whole, do not shine and generally rely on ice-cream or fruit with lashings of whipped cream to carry the day. Dutch pancakes *(flensjes* or *pannekoeken)* in all their dozens of varieties are good. To mention but one, which is a meal in itself, *spekpannekoek* is a pancake measuring about a foot across, and about half an inch thick. It should be loaded with bits of crisp, streaky bacon and be full of air pockets. It is served with fruit syrup or molasses. Three other favorites are *wafels met slagroom* (waffles with whipped cream), *poffertjes,* which can only be described as small lumps of dough, fried in butter and dusted with powdered sugar, but which the Dutch insist taste "as if an angel had caressed your tongue", and *spekkoek*—which literally means "bacon cake", probably because it looks like best-quality streaky bacon. The recipe comes from Indonesia and it consists of alternate layers of heavy butter sponge and spices. It tastes delicious and, besides fruit, is the only congruous dessert to a *rijsttafel,* a myriad of small dishes with rice.

Snacks—Nearly every town in Holland has many snack bars. Here you can get a *broodje* (roll) or sandwich in a hurry. These come in an infinite variety ranging from plain cheese to what amounts to a modest *hors d'oeuvre.* One of Holland's favorites is the *uitsmijter.* This is an open-face sandwich consisting of two fried eggs, laid on a foundation of ham, roast beef or cheese, on slices of buttered bread; potato and meat croquettes have recently become great favorites. The snack bars also offer several kinds of soup, cake, pastry, and ice-cream and some have a menu with two or three *plats du jour,* and to drink, tea, coffee, soft drinks, beer, and maybe wine. The service is usually fast and the cost modest.

What to Drink

Like the kitchen, Dutch bars are for the most part internationally-minded. First-class hotels and top restaurants in major cities have learned to make good martinis and similar cocktails. The indigenous drink, of course, is gin or *jenever*, a colorless, potent beverage that is served chilled, or at room temperature, in shot glasses and should be drunk neat as it does not mix well with any other liquid. Some Dutchmen drink it with cola or vermouth—but unless you have a very strong head avoid deviations. It comes in many varieties depending on the spices used, if any. *Jonge*, or young jenever, contains less sugar, is less creamy, but no less intoxicating than *oude*, or old, jenever. The *Bols* brand, still available in the famous stone crock which, when emptied of its original contents, was often used as a hot water bottle in wintertime, is best-known to most tourists, whereas the Dutch often prefer *Bokma*, although *De Kuyper* and *Claeryn* are also favored brands. If you don't like your gin straight try a *kleine angst* (literally little terror), which is a shot of young jenever with a liberal dash of angostura bitters. Don't gulp your jenever as the Dutch do—remember they're used to it! This innocuous, mild-tasting liquid has a delayed action which might have unfortunate results.

If you don't feel up to the challenge of tasting the Dutch water of life, they have an infinite choice. Besides the many kinds of sherry, vermouth, port and various beverages available in other countries, Holland offers a long list of gins—*bessen-jenever* (red-currant gin), *citroen-jenever* (lemon gin), and so forth, as well as *advocaat* (a heavier and creamier variety of eggnog).

Many Dutchmen drink beer with their meals. You'll make no mistake if you follow their example, because Dutch beer is good, always properly cooled and inexpensive. Imported Danish, English, Belgian and German beer is usually available, at about twice the price. Unless you want one of the heavier varieties just ask for a *pils*. Many breweries are open to the public. The famous Heineken brewing operations have moved to an industrial park in Zoeterwoude. The former brewery in Amsterdam is now a museum tracing the history of Dutch brewing. Write to the NBT for a complete list. Those in Limburg are particularly interesting, as they offer a variety of beers.

Better restaurants and hotel dining rooms will nearly always offer you a wine list.

Many nowadays serve a carafe or individual glasses of *vins du table* which is both palatable and reasonable. But where the wine lists are concerned the wines are generally good and with a wide range, and in comparison with other countries cannot be called expensive, except at the luxury hotels and restaurants.

Dutch liquers, on the other hand, are excellent and reasonable. *Curaçao* takes its name from the island of the same name in the Dutch West Indies. It receives its flavor from the peel of a special variety of orange grown there and is delicious. *Triple Sec* is almost the same thing as Cointreau, though a shade less subtle. *Parfait d'Amour* is a highly perfumed, amethyst-colored liqueur. Especially elegant, *goudwasser* (gold water), a clear sweetish liqueur, adorned with flecks of floating gold. Dutch-made ver-

sions of crême de menthe, apricot brandy, anisette, and similar liqueurs
are also very good.

Indonesian Cooking

Although Indonesian food tastes good at any time of the day, your digestion will probably appreciate it if you stick to lunch. The best restaurants are in Den Haag, Amsterdam and Rotterdam, although nearly all towns now have good ones. Throughout the country, many *Indisch-Chinese* restaurants also serve an Indonesian fare, but with a Chinese flavor. For authentic cuisine from the former Dutch colony, give preference to an *Indonesian* restaurant. In any case, it is always a good idea to have a chat with the manager, or the waiter, to get an explanation of what the dishes are composed of.

The most elaborate Indonesian meal is called a *rijsttafel*. This starts off prosaically enough with soup plates and a dish of plain, steamed rice. The rice serves as a foundation for the contents of anywhere from 15 to 50 dishes, each more delectable than the one before. Some of these are described below. Sit down to this in the mood to stuff yourself, be prepared to feel as if you want to go to bed and sleep it off afterwards (which is what most Dutchmen do) and don't be surprised if you feel hungry again a few hours later. If moderation is your virtue, try the less ambitious *nasi goreng* or *bami goreng* (fried rice or noodles—with choice bits of meat, shrimp, chicken and the like). These are equally delicious and make fewer demands on your palate.

An average *rijsttafel* is usually enough for two people, although you would do well to add one or two extra dishes from among these: *Saté babi,* bite-sized morsels of pork skewered on a wooden spit and cooked in a mouth-watering *pinda* (peanut) sauce, is delicious. *Loempia* is a mixture of bean sprouts and vegetables wrapped in wafer-like pastry and fried in deep oil. *Kroepoek* is a large, crunchy prawn-based cracker. Fried prawns are a welcome addition. *Daging* is the general name for stewed meat. *Daging smoor* identifies the kind prepared in a black sauce and is particularly delectable. *Daging roedjak, daging besengek,* and *daging oppor* identify variations prepared in red, green and white sauces, respectively. *Bebottok* is meat steamed in coconut milk. *Fricadel* is a forced meat ball, relatively bland and somewhat mushy. *Sambal ati* is liver stewed in a red sauce. *Sambal telor* is an egg in red sauce. *Sambal oedang* are shrimps in a red sauce. *Babi pangang* is pieces of delicious roast suckling pig in a mild spicy sauce.

Ajam (chicken) is served in as many ways as meat. *Sambalans* is a collective term for several varieties of stewed vegetables, some of which you have probably never seen before.

Seroendeng, fried coconut and peanuts, is also called *apenhaar* (monkey hair). *Gado gado* are cold vegetables in peanut sauce. *Atjar ketimoen* are cucumber sticks in vinegar. *Pisang goreng* are fried bananas. *Roedjak* is a compote of fresh fruit in a sweet sauce. *Sajor* means soup, and comes in a variety of guises, but is not a separate course as in most other countries.

To eat your *rijsttafel* you start off with a modest layer of rice on the bottom of your plate, adding a spoonful of each dish, arranging these neatly around the edge, finally filling in the center. It should be eaten with a spoon and fork. On a small dish you'll discover three or four little blobs of red and black paste—these are *sambals*. They are made of red peppers and spices and are generally red-hot. A little goes a long way. If you inadvertently bite into something that is painfully overspiced the remedy is a large spoonful of plain rice.

Beer, though not Indonesian, is the perfect beverage to accompany a *rijsttafel*. Jasmine tea, iced tea, lemonade or mineral water are also excellent. But never wine or milk.

Final Reminders

In nearly all Dutch restaurants, whether the cuisine be French, Indonesian or Serbo-Croatian, a service charge of 15 percent and a Value Added Tax (VAT) are included in the bill. This also applies to a *borrel* (a shot of Dutch gin) or any other drink in a bar or café. If you have any doubts, ask. Unless the service has been unusually attentive, you're at perfect liberty to pocket all your change, just as the average Dutchman does.

Remember, too, that the better Dutch restaurants are fairly formal. If you prefer casual dress at mealtime, pick a modest type of place or you'll feel awkward matching your sportswear against the headwaiter's white tie and tails. The better Dutch restaurants hardly ever have high chairs or children's portions, so the youngest members of your party will likely fare better at your hotel.

Because the Dutch follow the continental custom of relaxing at the table, allow at least an hour for a simple meal, two for something more elaborate. When short of time (or money) but brave enough to try a really cheap meal, try your hand at one of the "automatieks." A guilder or two in the slot and you pull out: a *kroketje*—a croquette with either veal or beef; a *loempia*—Chinese/Indonesian pancake roll; a *gehaktbal*—meat ball; a *nasischijf* or *bamihap*—Indonesian-version meat ball, rather hot, with rice or noodles; a *huzarensalade*—Russian salad (cold hard-boiled egg with lettuce leaf, slice of tomato, gherkin).

If you intend to eat something at an automatiek, take care to have some guilders, as only some have change machines and it is not always possible to get your money changed.

All in all, eating is a delight in Holland, especially as nowadays there is no difficulty in finding places to suit every palate or fancy. True, it is expensive in most places, but the personal attention and service are often worth it. Moreover, a growing number of restaurants all over the country now serve the so-called tourist menu, which provides more than enough food for the average visitor (the Dutch themselves have tremendous appetites), and at a price about half the normal menu rates. So if you are traveling on a budget, look out for the notices which announce "Tourist Menu," which is priced, by law, at about Fl. 21 for three courses. Alternatively try a restaurant that has a "Dutch-French Menu," "Romantic Menu," or "Gourmet Menu" (details from the NBT).

In many towns the street carts and stalls serve a variety of food. Herrings, to be eaten with the fingers, sandwiches, and *broodjes*—rolls containing cheese, meat, or fish, often with salad—are the most common. Another speciality is *bollen,* deep fried balls of crispy batter, usually formed around fruit centres.

The visitor is unlikely to leave Holland hungry or slimmer. It can, in fact, be a real problem for anyone on a strict diet!

SHOPPING

From Diamonds and Delft to Cheese and Cigars

The question of what to take home as a souvenir of the Netherlands has as many facets as one of the glittering Amsterdam diamonds. If your purse and luggage are limited, you can always tuck a piece of pewter into your suitcase, or an antique *koekeplank* (cookie mould) carved with amusing designs. Other possibilities in the same category include pretty enamel ashtrays, blue-and-white Delftware, crystal from Leerdam or Maastricht, a Gouda cheese, striped aprons from Marken, or a box of those delicious hard candies called *Haagse Hopjes*.

Holland has a wide range of markets. In Amsterdam alone, there are flea markets, a bird market, stamp and book markets, art, antiques, textiles, and flower markets. Avid shoppers can write to the Amsterdam VVV for their excellent pamphlets about shopping in the city, covering many walking tours linked to different shopping themes, from fashion to arts and crafts.

Amsterdam is the logical place to start for most tourists, although Den Haag, thanks to the presence of the diplomatic colony as well as the European headquarters of many international companies, can offer almost as wide and varied a selection. Venturing farther afield, Haarlem, Delft, Leiden, and in fact, almost every town can also be interesting, as they frequently have more "local" antiques at prices lower than in the large cities. It is astonishing to see the wealth of antique treasures still in Holland, and although many of these come from other countries, some of them are genuinely Dutch, while the remainder can almost always be relied on to be authentic articles from elsewhere. The shops tend to be localized in particular streets or districts, making it easy to shop-hop.

Further, many places like Den Haag or Breda, for example, have antique markets in the town center during summer. These are generally supervised by the local authorities, although of course, no guarantee is given about authenticity. Still, many a good bargain, Dutch and foreign, can be picked up in these marketplaces. Prices are usually reasonable and a little bargaining occasionally makes them more so. Details of the locations of these markets will be found under the Practical Information sections at the end of each regional chapter.

Amsterdam, Home of the Diamond Cutters

During the Middle Ages, Antwerp was Europe's great diamond center. After the Spanish conquest of 1576, many diamond experts fled north to Amsterdam. During the latter part of the 17th century, master gem-cutters from persecuted religious groups all over the Continent found refuge in Amsterdam. This, timed with the discovery of Brazilian diamond fields, gave the industry a tremendous boost. At the French court of Louis XV, brilliants were in high demand to set off powdered wigs. In those days, facets were made by rubbing two diamonds together on a wheel turned by women. Violent protest was voiced by the fairer sex in 1822 when horse-power began replacing feminine hands. At that time, when a shipload of raw diamonds arrived from India or Brazil, there was feverish activity for several months until the cargo was cut and the finished stones sent, with Paris the principal destination, to be sold. Then factories stood idle until a new shipment landed.

Political upheavals throughout Europe during the latter part of the 19th century caused a serious crisis in the diamond industry. Unexpectedly, it was saved by children of a Dutch farmer living near Hopetown, South Africa, who discovered that the pebbles in a nearby stream made marvelous toys. For 500 sheep, 10 oxen, and one horse, one of these twinkling marbles representing 21 carats, found its way to Europe. The diamond rush was on and Kimberley, South Africa, became the big center. In 1870, the first shipment of South African diamonds reached Europe, commencing a trade that today supplies 90 per cent of the world's diamonds.

A visit to one of the modern diamond centers in Amsterdam offers the visitor a brief education in this fascinating business. You will see a demonstration with glass dummies which shows how the diamond is mined, cut, and polished. It is a process which fascinatingly combines modern techniques with the kind of skill only learned through many generations of craftsmen. First, each diamond is examined by experts to determine its exact color, weight, grain, and possible flaws. Then it is decided how it should be cut. Later, the finished product is scrutinized for quality and price. One of the great triumphs of the diamond cutter's art was the work on the world's largest diamond (the Cullinan), which represented over 3,000 carats when it was discoverd in Transvaal in 1905 and presented to King Edward VII of England. After months of study, the fabulous stone was split to make the world's largest polished diamond. It was set in the crown of England. Another massive gem from the same stone was placed in the royal scepter and two more have been mounted in a pin for Queen Elizabeth II. The smallest in the world was also cut here as a demonstration of master technique. It weighed ¼ of a milligram; or 1/2,500,000 of the Cullinan.

We are told that it takes an entire day to saw one carat. Next comes the cleaving or shaping by hand, followed by the important polishing process, which gives the diamond its 58 different facets. You will notice that the size of a gem is usually proportionate to the number of grey hairs on the head of its worker, for it takes 15 years of experience to know how to polish the big stuff. The untrained eye can tell a good diamond at one glance by its blue-white color, although there is also a current craze for black diamonds. You could do worse than to choose a sparkling diamond as a life-long souvenir of your visit to Holland—it will cost less than elsewhere. There is also an excellent diamond store in the duty-free Shopping Center at Schiphol Airport, but do not buy before immersing yourself in the polishing techniques on display in the better diamond houses in Amsterdam.

Solid Dutch Silver

Silver is considered to be another good buy in Holland. The metallic content of its products is guaranteed by special controlling marks. The marks consist of a lion and number, indicating the purity of the silver, either .925 (sterling quality) or the more usual .833, to which may be added the town and maker's mark. Much antique silver was also stamped with the coat of arms of the city of its origin and sometimes the guild mark of its maker.

For example, three crosses topped by a crown was the mark of old Amsterdam, while a stork was the mark used by silversmiths in Den Haag. Indeed by law all Dutch silver must be hallmarked, which makes buying modern silver much easier, but the knowledge of marks on old pieces is a specialized business and one that should be researched very carefully; otherwise, it's best to buy from a reputable dealer, who will explain, and should guarantee, its origin.

A number of museums, large and small, feature collections of fine old silver. Notable are the display in Amsterdam's Rijksmuseum and in the Fries Museum in Leeuwarden or in the Nederlands Goud, Zilver en Klokkenmuseum in Schoonhoven.

The Dutch silver industry in Voorschoten started about 100 years ago in a small shed. It is now known as Van Kempen & Begeer and an enlarged factory stands there on this firm's private property. For silver filigree work and embossed plaques, the Dutch government has set up a school for the cultivation of fine silversmiths and goldsmiths in Schoonhoven.

In recent years a large trade has been built up in Holland in English and Continental silver, especially tea and coffee services, candelabra, and Victorian and Georgian tableware. Prices are admittedly high, but for visitors to Europe who cannot include a trip to England in their itinerary, this sort of souvenir can often be a good buy. All the large Dutch jewelers' shops carry extensive stocks of this old silver.

When looking for not too expensive jewelery as souvenirs, ask to be shown rings, bracelets or brooches and tie-pins with the traditional *Zeeuwse knop* or Zeeland knob pattern: a silver filigree rosette. They make an unusual, original, and not too pricey gift.

Delve into Delft

Most gift counters, hotel lobbies, and china shops are littered with so-called Delftware, much of it mass produced by factories in Gouda. The art of making the authentic blue-and-white earthenware, however, is not extinct.

In the 17th century, 30 different potteries produced Delft china. Now there are only two, of which the Royal Factory at Delft is the most famous. Founded in 1653, it bears the worthy name of De Porceleyne Fles. On the bottom of each object that is produced a triple signature appears: a plump vase topped by a straight line, the stylized letter *F* below it, and the word Delft. The only discernible difference between a new piece of hand-painted Delft and an old one is age. Genuine Delft may be recognized by its color, the fine shine of its glaze, the complexity of its design, and the superlative way it is expressed. The varying shades of blue found in Delft depend on the particular artist. Small scattered leaves known as the parsley pattern are characteristic of many of its pieces. The big floral splotches or simple portraits without detail are usually produced by practicing beginners.

The price of a genuine Delft article is never determined by its size but by the quality of its painting. As every object is hand-drawn, unaided by stencils or tracings, the quantity is exceedingly limited. You can understand that an entire Delft dinner service is rare; it becomes too expensive for the buyer as well as an interminable bore for the artist to complete. Visitors are welcome at De Porceleyne Fles in Delft (Rotterdamseweg 196; open daily) to see its showroom of exquisite museum pieces as well as demonstrations with the potter's wheel, the oven, and the brush. Although blue and white Delft sprinkled with floral bouquets is the most popular, other variations of Delftware do exist.

The milk-white ware, without design, was exclusively for kitchen use during the 17th century. However, in 1936 a small white collection of ridged, petal-edged decorative pieces was started, using the old moulds. Recently, a new line of white has been introduced, featuring sleek smooth forms to suit modern interiors. Also keeping step with the present is an entirely original conception of Delft that alternates black with earthy tones of gray and brown in unusual futuristic shapes, decorated by Wynblad-inspired etchings of people scratched into the glaze, rather than painted below it.

In 1948, a rich red cracked glaze was introduced depicting profuse flowers, graceful birds, and leaping gazelles. (The special cracked texture of this pottery is achieved only after six or seven bakings.) A range of green, gold, and black known as New-Delft is exquisitely drawn with minuscule figures to resemble an old Persian tapestry.

The marvelous Pynacker Delft borrowing Japanese motifs dominated by rich orange with gold, deep blue, and touches of green, has existed since the 17th century. The brighter Polychrome Delft carries a bolder picture in sun-flower yellow, vivid orange, and blue with green suggestions.

Magnificent reproductions of canvases made by 17th-century artists are executed on circular dishes in blue or brown sepia. For a goodish price, you can have your portrait drawn on a Delft plate. De Porceleyne Fles even produces a limited number of unpainted, specially glazed tiles for industrial uses in buildings, bathrooms, and swimming pools.

A commemorative tile or wall-plate could well provide that "different" present. Of the many designs for a new baby, there is one with the child's name, place, and date of birth encircling a grandfather clock, denoting the hour and the minute, and a cradle. Dutch *jenever* and liqueurs, too, bottled in blue-and-white Delftware jugs or Gouda china dolls in national costume make attractive gifts. These items, of course, along with many of the so-called Delft tiles, are found everywhere in souvenir shops, and are seldom made in Delft.

There are, indeed, several Dutch makes of pottery which make good souvenirs. Some have much the same design and color as Delft and are usually somewhat cheaper, while others have their own distinctive designs. The name of the maker is always given on the bottom of the piece, so there is no risk of mistaking it for Delft or any make of English or Continental pottery. In addition to the better known Delft wares, attractive traditional and folk designs of pottery are found in some of the smaller towns, such as Makkum—especially worth a visit—and Workum, in Friesland.

Pewter Pots and Plates, Crystal

During the 17th century, pewter was a necessary complement to Delft blue plates. However, age is no guarantee that the pewter you unearth in an antique shop is fine. Three hundred years ago, they made bad pewter just as they do today. Cast in old moulds, Meeuws' handwrought pewter tends to retain the original shapes you see pictured in the museums. Pewter is a mixture of tin and lead. The greater lead content a piece contains, the more worthless it becomes . . . bending easily, tarnishing quickly, and denting without apparent cause. Don't be misled by the bright appearance of those long necked jugs you see in the knickknack shops around town. Look for the heavy duty quality, preferably Meeuws' if it is new, with only five percent lead and an eternal shine.

Leerdam crystal has become famous for its fine design and lovely blue-white color. The forms vary from wide-mouthed champagne glasses balanced on cut stems to generous cornucopian vases to elegant glittery candlesticks to chubby beer beakers. Ask any reliable glass shop to let you see a complete catalogue of stocks and styles. Maastricht crystal, though as beautiful as Leerdam, is generally less expensive. Heavier, more cut and worked, it often resembles the French Baccarat while its competitor to the north can be compared to Swedish Orrefors.

Dutch cigars are always a good buy as gifts, but bear in mind your Customs quota.

If you do not want to carry cheeses home with you, you might find that cheese accessories such as cutting boards with small glass domes, or specially designed knives, make very acceptable souvenirs.

When you want to take home a pair of clogs, do NOT buy them at a souvenir shop but ask for them when in the country, where the farmers buy them. You'll get them for a much lower price and there will be more choice.

Eatables, Drinkables and Plantables

The Dutch love to eat and drink and their favorite foods provide splendid opportunities for souvenir and gift shopping. Dutch cheeses and the potent *jenever* gin are obvious choices, but Holland also produces a wide range of liqueurs such as *Curaçao,* or *Advocaat,* a type of eggnog, and many flavored with fruit or herbs. Dutch chocolate and a variety of specialized candies cater to those with a sweet tooth, while pickled herring, or smoked eel, are delicious savoury souvenirs.

The bulbfields of Holland are among the country's top scenic attractions, and their products are ideal as gifts to take home. One word of warning, here, on the regulations applied by some countries to imports of plants, which may limit the type or quantity of such produce that can be taken home, but commercial growers offering plants or bulbs for sale can advise on these regulations for most countries and will supply appropriate purchases. It is usually easier, even advisable, to let the shops ship the bulbs, for a small extra charge, to their final destination.

A Last Word

If you are leaving the Netherlands by air it might be useful to remember that the tax-free shops at both Schiphol (Amsterdam) and Rotterdam Airports, open for long hours, offer a mouth-watering display of cameras, watches, liquors, tobacco, perfume, jewelry, toys, porcelain, and the flower bulbs and seed for which Holland is so justly famous, at prices which are often lower than in the ordinary shops. Since the standard of duty-free shops around the world is so variable, many of them being far more expensive than the stores just around the corner from you at home, it is a pleasure to be able to record that Schiphol has been voted the best duty-free shopping center in Europe in an extensive survey of independent travelers.

AMSTERDAM

City of a Thousand and One Bridges

Nearly 1,000 years ago, so the legend goes, two fishermen and their dog beached their boat on a sandbank where the river Amstel flowed into the IJ, the old Dutch word for water. They settled there, prospered and were joined by others. The village was named after the river and the dam that had been built there: Amstelledamme.

By 1275 Amstelledamme had grown sufficiently to be awarded a city charter, and its prosperity continued to increase over the next 200 years. But it was the fall of Antwerp, in what is today Belgium, to Spain in 1576 that provided the major spur to the city's growth. Most of Antwerp's merchants moved north to Amsterdam, bringing their wealth and trading connections.

The city embarked on a period of rapid expansion and fast-growing prosperity. Trade was the cornerstone of the city's success. Indeed so successful were the city's merchants, that by 1600 their merchant fleet was larger than those of all the rest of the Low Countries combined. Following the establishment of the East India Company in 1602, the city rose to the peak of its influence, and its ships were seen in every corner of the globe. The Bank of Amsterdam, one of the oldest in the world, was established in 1609.

The key to this spectacular mercantile success story was water, or, to be more exact, the canal system, which remains one of the city's most prominent features. The first canals had been built essentially as defensive moats, but by 1600 they came to be used for trading purposes. The building of the Herengracht, Keizersgracht and Prinsengracht canals in the city center which started in 1612, was the first step in turning the city into a vast port. More were gradually added, until the beginning of the 18th century, so that it was possible to unload cargoes in the heart of the city direct from the ships that had carried them there.

By then much of the city's center had assumed its present day appearance. Many of the houses whose upper stories were used for storing this flood of tea, spices, silks, and furs can still be seen. The heavy beams that jut out from their topmost gables lack only a rope and the men to pull it; the patrician mansions seem still to echo with the steps of the "burghers" whose portraits were painted by Rembrandt and Frans Hals.

Water was the city's nemesis as well. Twice during the 17th century the locks were opened and the surrounding countryside flooded in defense against the attacks of Prince Willem II and Louis XIV. In January, 1795, however, the stratagem failed when the temperature fell and the waters froze, thus enabling Napoleon's cavalry to ride across the ice and capture the proud city for France. Even before this time, moreover, the Zuiderzee had begun to silt up. Only ships with flat bottoms and relatively shallow draft could clear the mudbanks, and this during an era when the British were learning to construct stout, deep-keeled vessels that could carry twice the cargo of a Dutch boat twice as fast. Commerce stagnated from the late 17th century until the completion of the North Holland Canal in 1825 and the North Sea Canal in 1876, while England supplanted Holland as mistress of the seas.

The Spanish also had a hand in making Amsterdam great. Not only did they suppress rival Antwerp but the dreaded Inquisition drove out liberal Catholics, Protestants, and Jews alike, many of whom settled in Holland's leading city where religious toleration and freedom of conscience also attracted certain Separatists or Pilgrims from England, some of whom in 1620 set sail for the Americas where they founded Plymouth, Massachusetts. After the revocation of the Edict of Nantes, these Flemish, Spanish, Portuguese and English refugees were joined by French Protestants. Most of the families who sought asylum in Amsterdam were hardworking, thrifty and skilled in trade, craft or industry. Their talents, their money, and their gratitude to the city that had made them welcome had a catalytic effect on the Dutch themselves and their surroundings.

Today, Amsterdam is a bustling, vigorous city. It is the capital of the Netherlands and with its new suburban agglomeration, has a population of about one million. The fourth greatest European tourist attraction, after Rome, London and Paris, it celebrated its 700th birthday in 1975.

Exploring Amsterdam

By whatever means you arrive in Amsterdam you will be struck by the symmetrical rings of canals and the 1,200 bridges lacing them together. There are 160 canals lined by some 7,000 buildings, many dating from the 16th to the 18th centuries. They are the most characteristic features of this delightful bourgeois city whose character is indelibly stamped with the taste and philosophy of the early 17th century. Time has vindicated its builders, and if few of the stately patrician houses are still owned by merchant princes, few have been allowed to fall into disrepair.

A glance at the map confirms the relatively ordered layout of Amsterdam's heart. Imagine a horizontal line with a dip in its middle. The left-hand side of the line is the North Sea Canal, an engineering accomplishment of the first magnitude that cuts a 15-mile swath through what was once sand dunes to provide a direct outlet to the ocean. The right-hand side of the line is the IJ River (pronounced "eye"), which once flowed into the brackish Zuiderzee and thence into the North Sea by a round-about route that led north past Hoorn, Enkhuizen, and Den Oever. Today, of course, the Zuiderzee is a fresh-water lake called the IJsselmeer in honor of this selfsame river. Along both sides of this line is a complex of piers, harbors, drydocks, warehouses, cranes, and other maritime facilities that testify to Amsterdam's importance as a center of world trade.

The dip in the middle of our hypothetical line marks the point at which an artificial island was built to receive the Central Station (1889), whose elaborate towers and cluttered façade were designed by Cuypers in a style that is euphemistically called Dutch Renaissance. The medieval core of Amsterdam, marked by a confusion of waterways that have since been partially filled in (Damrak and Rokin were once canals), is directly below this dip and thus within a few minutes' walk of the station itself. Around this core you'll notice four semicircular rings of canals, with two more at a somewhat greater distance. Planted with elms and lined with gabled, red-brick mansions and storehouses, they are best explored on foot. We seriously advise you to do your exploring with map in hand. The concentrically circular nature of the city's layout makes it easy to start walking in exactly the opposite direction from the one you thought you were going.

A favorite itinerary takes about an hour and follows the east or inner side of the Herengracht from the Raadhuisstraat (behind the Dam and the Royal Palace) to the south and then the east as far as Thorbeckeplein and Reguliersgracht. Americans may wish to detour briefly to the building at Keizersgracht 529, where John Adams lived for two years (1780–82) when he first arrived in the Netherlands. His son John Quincy studied at the Latin School on the Singel. During Adam's stay, he negotiated $2 million in loans from the wealthy banking family who lived at Singel 460 (now a dance hall) for the infant United States. Other loans from this and other houses soon followed to a total of $30 million, a generous Dutch gesture of confidence in the future of America.

From the Central Station to the Dam

As you emerge from the Central Station, the Haarlemmerstraat lies just to the right. A tablet at No. 75 (now the site of the John Adams Foundation) commemorates the occasion in 1623 when the directors of the Dutch West India Company planned the founding of Nieuw Amsterdam on the southernmost tip of the island of "Manhattes." Two years later the first permanent settlement was made, followed in 1626 by the purchase of a good part of the island from the native Indians "for the value of 60 guilders." In 1664, the colony was seized by the English and renamed New York.

The street directly opposite the station is Prins Hendrikkade, where Sinterklaas arrives in November. A new hotel behind the restored gable facades, adjacent to the St. Nicolaaskerk, is part of a city scheme to rejuvenate the waterfront.

About a block farther along the Prins Hendrikkade is the tower of the Schreierstoren (the Criers' Tower or Weeping Tower), where seafarers used to say goodbye to their women before setting off to faraway places. At the angle of Geldersekade and Oudezijdskolk, it was erected in 1487 and a tablet marks the point from which Henry Hudson set sail in the *Half Moon* on April 4, 1609 on a voyage that took him to what is now New York and the river that bears his name. The "Weeping Tower" is now used as a combined reception and exposition center that includes a bookshop selling maritime books.

A right turn onto the Oude Zijds Voorburgwal brings you to the oldest part of the city. Close by, at Oudekerplein, is the Oude Kerk, or Old Church, consecrated in 1306, now in the heart of the red light district. Although badly damaged by iconoclasts after the Reformation, the church retains its original belltower and a few remarkable stained glass windows. From the tower, there is a good view of this ancient part of the city. Also its organ, made most famous by the late 16th-century composer Jan Sweelinck, who is buried in the church, as is Rembrandt's wife Saskia. The lovely carillon (complex set of bells) are also worth taking in. During the summer organ concerts are held on Tuesday, Wednesday, Friday and Saturday evening.

Another few steps at Oudezijds Voorburgwal 40 is the Amstelkring Museum whose façade carries the inscription "Ons' Lieve Heer Op Solder" or "Our Dear Lord In The Attic." In 1578 Amsterdam embraced Protestantism and, just as reformist sects had previously been forbidden by Catholicism, forbade the Church of Rome. So great was the tolerance of the municipal authorities, however, that clandestine Catholic chapels were allowed to exist as long as their activities were reasonably discreet. At one time, there were 62 such institutions in Amsterdam alone. One such was installed in 1663 in the attics of three separate houses built around 1661, whose lower floors were ordinary dwellings. It was in use until 1887, the year that the St. Nicolaaskerk opposite the Central Station was consecrated for Catholic worship, since which time the hidden church has been preserved by both Protestant and Catholic owners as a monument to toleration in the midst of bigotry. Of interest are the baroque altar with its revolving tabernacle, the swinging pulpit that can be stowed out of sight, the upstairs gallery, and the display cases in some of the rooms. Organ recitals are sometimes given here at 4 o'clock on Sunday afternoons.

Returning to the Damrak, the broad thoroughfare that leads towards the Dam from the Central Station, we pass the piers of excursion boats and reach the former Beurs or Exchange, designed by Berlage, now an exhibition center and concert hall.

If you continue east another two or three blocks, you pass through the red-light district, known as the *walletjes* or *rosse buurt*. The area is generally safe, but midnight walks down dark side-streets are not advisable!

The Dam and the Koninklijk Paleis

Instead of turning aside, however, let's continue up the Damrak to the Dam, the broadest square in the old section of town. To the left you'll note the simple monument to Dutch victims of World War II. The 12 urns contain soil from the 11 provinces and from the former Dutch East Indies, now Indonesia. The old name for this part of the Square is Vischmarkt

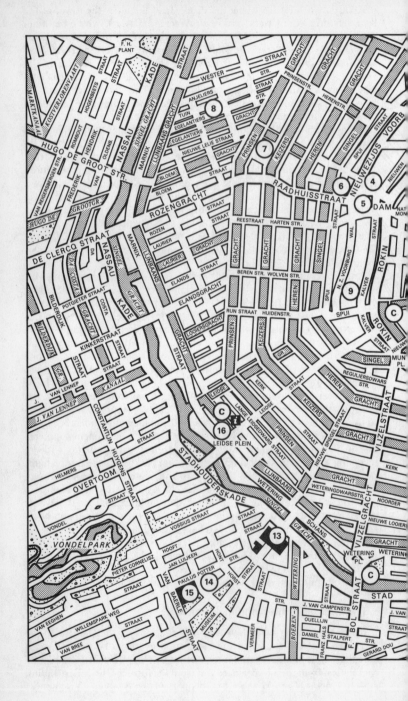

AMSTERDAM

1 Central Station
2 St. Nicolaaskerk
3 Oude Kerk (Old Church)
4 Nieuwe Kerk (New Church)
5 Koninklijk Paleis (Royal Palace)
6 Telecom Huis (Main
  Telecommunications Center)
7 Anne Frank Huis
8 Joordan District
9 Amsterdam Historisch Museum
10 Zuiderkerk (South Church)
11 Museum het Rembrandthuis
12 Zoological Gardens
13 Rijksmuseum
14 Rijksmuseum Vincent Van Gogh
15 Stedelijk Museum (Municipal Museum)
16 Stadsschouwburg (Theater)
17 Joods Museum
18 Muziek Theatre/City Hall
19 Main Post Office
   Canal Trips - starting points
   VVV Tourist Information Offices

(Fishmarket) where the boats of the fishing fleet would come in and sell their catch; today it is busy with shops, people, and traffic. It is also a popular center for outdoor concerts. To the northwest of the Dam is the Nieuwe Kerk, New Church. Dating originally from around 1400, it was expanded gradually until approximately 1490 when it reached its present size. Gutted by fire in 1645, it was reconstructed in imposing Renaissance style (as interpreted by strict Calvinists). The superb oak pulpit, the great organ (1645), the monumental tomb of Admiral de Ruyter, the stained glass windows and the great organ (1645) are all shown to great effect on national holidays, when the church is bedecked with flowers. As befits Holland's national church, it is the site of all coronations; Queen Beatrix was inaugurated here in 1980. The church is also used as a meeting place, and is home to a lively cafe, temporary exhibitions, and concerts. Built into the north porch of the church are two of the smallest shops in Europe: if one customer enters, the shop is full.

The Koninklijk Paleis (Royal Palace) or Dam Palace, a vast, well-proportioned structure completed in 1655, was built originally to replace the city hall that had stood on the same site but had burned down. Remarkably, it is built on 13,659 piles, an excellent illustration of the problems posed by building on the marshy soil of this part of Holland. The great pedimental sculptures are an allegorical representation of Amsterdam surrounded by Neptune and mythological sea-creatures. The seven archways at street level symbolize the then seven provinces of the Netherlands, although the entrance, oddly enough, is on the opposite side of the building. In 1808 it was converted into a palace for Louis Bonaparte, Napoleon's brother, who abdicated two years later. Theoretically, it is now the official residence of Queen Beatrix, but she seldom uses it, preferring to live at Huis ten Bosch in Den Haag. The Dam Palace now sees only an occasional reception for a visiting Head of State and the Queen's annual New Year reception of the whole diplomatic corps. Parts of the palace are open to the public. Opening times vary so check with VVV office.

Behind the palace is the ornate former post office, now being converted into a shopping complex. From here the Raadhuisstraat leads west across three canals to the Westermarkt and the Westerkerk, or West Church, built in 1631 by Pieter de Keyser to plans drawn up by his father, Hendrick (who was also responsible for the Zuiderkerk and Noorderkerk). Its 275-ft. tower, the highest in the city, has a large Emperor's crown commemorating Maximilian of Austria at its summit. It also houses an outstanding carillon. Rembrandt and his son Titus are buried here (lying side by side), and Queen Beatrix was married here. During the summer, one can climb the tower for a fine view over the city.

Opposite, at number six Westermarkt, Descartes, the great French 17th-century philosopher *(Cogito, ergo sum)* lived for a brief period in 1634. The house is identified by a commemorative plaque. Another, more famous house, is found on the adjacent Prinsengracht. This is the Anne Frank Huis, immortalized in the immensely moving diary kept by the young Anne Frank from 1942 to 1944. The Franks, a German-Jewish family, had emigrated to Amsterdam in 1933, following Hitler's rise to power. They managed to evade the Nazis for over two years after the invasion of Holland in May 1940, before moving into the house in July 1942. Here they hid in empty, barren rooms, reached by a small, cleverly-disguised passage leading off the library, and here Anne kept her record of two increasingly fraught years before their capture and deportation to Auschwitz. A small exhibition of the Holocaust can also be found in the house.

From the Dam you can also turn into the Kalverstraat, a popular shopping street favored by the young, which leads south from the left-hand side of the palace. At No. 92 is the beautiful Renaissance (1581) gate of the former Burgerweeshuis or City Orphanage, which has another entrance around the corner to the right in St. Luciensteeg (1634). The first was for boys, the second for girls. The inner court dates from about 1670. The black and red coloring in the coat of arms of Amsterdam was reflected in the uniforms of the orphans; they had one red and one black sleeve. In medieval times, this whole area was an island devoted to piety. Although the bordering canals are now filled in, the spot remains a place apart.

This historic site now houses Historisch Museum, which was enlarged and enriched for the 700th anniversary celebrations of the city in 1975. The museum traces the history of Amsterdam from its humble origins as a fishing village to the 17th-century "Golden Age" of material and artistic wealth and on to the decline of the country's trading empire in the 18th century. There are maps, documents, plans, and works of art. The restaurant adjoining the courtyard is a good spot for lunch.

Continue down Kalverstraat, turn right into Begijnsteeg, and continue to the delightful Begijnhof, which boasts one of the two remaining authentic Gothic facades in Amsterdam. If this door is not open, go around the corner to Spui and the main entrance gate. Founded in 1346, the houses enclosing the original courtyard date mainly from the 17th century. They were occupied by Beguines, pious women from good families who chose to devote their lives to works of charity. The women often took a vow of chastity but kept their personal possessions. The last Beguine died in 1974; her house (number 26) has been preserved as she left it. Number 34, which dates from the 15th century and is one of the oldest homes in Amsterdam, is the only one with its original wooden Gothic facade. Many of the gabled brick houses retain their beamed ceilings and stone tablets, which are engraved with Biblical scenes.

In the center of the square is a church given to Amsterdam's English and Scottish Presbyterians more than 300 years ago. On the church wall and also in the chancel are tributes to the Pilgrim Fathers, who sailed from Delftshaven to the New World in 1620. Opposite the church is another of the city's "secret" Catholic chapels, housed in a building that dates from 1671.

Muntplein to Rembrandt's House

Once back in Kalverstraat, you soon come to Spui, a lively square in the heart of the university area. It was a center for student rallies in revolutionary 1968. Now it is a center for partying in the ubiquitous "brown cafés".

The magnificent shuttered brick building at 423 Singel (by the canal) is a former artillery warehouse (1606), now the library for the University of Amsterdam.

Walk past it and take the next left onto Heiligeweg (Holy Road), back to Kalverstraat, turn right, and continue to the Muntplein with its 1620 Munttoren or Mint Tower, a graceful structure whose clock and bells still

seem to mirror the Golden Age. Cross the bridge and stroll through the
flower market on Singel canal.

From the Singel, take Leidsestraat to the Herengracht, the city's most
prestigious canal. The stretch of canal from here to Huidenstraat is named
"The Golden Bend" for its sumptuous patrician houses with double staircases and grand entrances. Seventeenth century merchants moved here
from the Amstel River to escape the disadvantages of their wealth; the
noisy warehouses; the unpleasant smells from the breweries; and the risk
of fire in the sugar refineries. These houses display the full range of Amsterdam facades: "neck", "bell" and "step" gables next door to grander
Louis XIV-style houses with elaborate cornices, double staircases and frescoed ceilings. In particular, look at numbers 364–370 as well as number
380 with its sculpted angels and Louis XIV facade. Numbers 390 and 392
display neck-shaped gables surmounted by statues of a couple in matching
17th-century dress. These houses are best seen from the east side of the
canal. For more gables, turn left down Wolvenstraat into the Keizersgracht, the Emperor's Canal.

Alternatively, take the Museum Boat or the metro to Waterlooplein and
walk east to Jodenbreestraat. This is the heart of *Jodenbuurt,* the old Jewish district, an important area to all Amsterdammers. At number four is
the house where Rembrandt lived from 1639 to 1658, now the Museum
Het Rembrandthuis. It was built in 1606, originally with only two stories.
The ground floor was used for living quarters, the upper floor was Rembrandt's studio. For three years, Rembrandt and his wife Saskia lived here
in considerable pomp. But following the death of Saskia in 1642, the great
man became increasingly introspective and his business gradually declined, though his output remained as prodigious as ever. Finally, in 1658
he was forced to sell the house to meet the demands of a multitude of credi-
tors, and with his mistress Hendrijke Stoffels, who had originally been his
housekeeper, and son Titus, moved to the much less prestigious Rozengracht, beyond the Westermarkt. The house, on the Jodenbreestraat, was
acquired by the city in 1906, and opened as a museum five years later.
It is fascinating to visit, both as a record of life in 17th-century Amsterdam
and of the life and working methods of one of Holland's presiding genius-
es. It contains a superb collection of Rembrandt's etchings. From St. An-
tonies Sluis bridge just by the house, there is a canal view little changed
since Rembrandt's time.

As the name Jodenbreestraat suggests, Rembrandt's house was located
in the midst of Amsterdam's Jewish quarter. The original settlers were
wealthy Sephardic Jews from Spain and Portugal, later followed by poorer
Ashkenazic refugees from Germany and Poland. At the turn of the century, this was a thriving community of Jewish diamond polishers, dyers and
merchants. During the Second World War, the corner of Jodenbreestraat
marked the end of *Joodse wijk,* (neighborhood), by then an imposed ghet-
to. Modern flats (apartments), built since 1965, when the old homes were
demolished to make way for the metro, have destroyed the original character of the street. Neighboring Muiderstraat has more character. Notice
the gateways decorated with pelicans, symbolizing great love since, according to legend, the pelican will feed her starving young with her own
blood. Close by, at Waterlooplein 41, the Portuguese Jew and philosopher
Baruch Spinoza was born in 1632.

Visserplein is a square linking Jodenbreestraat with Muiderstraat. In the center is a burly statue of a Dockwerker (docker), a significant part of city history. The statue commemorates the 1942 strike when Amsterdammers expressed their solidarity with persecuted Jews. A memorial march is held on February 25th every year. Facing the docker is the 17th-century Portuguese Synagogue. As one of Amsterdam's four neighboring synagogues, it was part of the largest Jewish religious complex in Europe. The austere interior is still intact, if marooned on a traffic island.

On the other side of the street is the Jewish Historical Museum, set in the complex of three ancient synagogues. These synagogues once served a population of 100,000 Jews, shrunk to under 10,000 after the atrocities of the Second World War. The museum, founded by American and Dutch Jews, displays religious treasures in a clear cultural and historical context. Since the synagogues lost most of their treasures during the war, it is their architecture and history that are the most compelling testaments.

You can catch the Museum Boat from Blauwbrug on Waterlooplein to the Central Station or to a destination near your hotel. If you'd rather walk, stroll along Nieuwe Herengracht. In Rembrandt's day, there were views of distant windjammers sailing into port; today the canal is full of permanently moored houseboats.

Amsterdam's Museum Quarter

Over the bridge and to the right, just a few minutes' walk from the Leidseplein, you'll find three of the most distinguished museums in Holland—the Rijksmuseum, the Stedelijk Museum and the Rijksmuseum Vincent van Gogh. Of the three, the Rijksmuseum, easily recognized by its cluster of towers, is the most important. It was founded originally by Louis Bonaparte in 1808, but the present rather lavish building dates from 1885. The museum contains significant collections of furniture, textiles, ceramics, sculpture and prints, as well as Italian, Flemish and Spanish paintings, many of the highest quality. But the great pride of the Rijksmuseum is its collection of 16th- and 17th-century Dutch paintings, a collection unmatched by any other in the world.

Perhaps the single most famous painting is Rembrandt's *The Night Watch*, commissioned by the Company of Captain Cocq and Lieutenant van Ruytenburg and completed in 1642. The picture was originally even larger than it is today (a spectacular 14 by 12 feet). But in 1775 it was transferred to the War Council in what is today the Royal Palace, and it was necessary to cut 26 inches from the width and 11 from the height. The title of the picture is actually rather misleading. It was long assumed, quite naturally, that Rembrandt's dark and mysterious picture represented a night scene. In fact, it was only when the painting was cleaned in 1947 that it became clear that it was a daytime picture. Nonetheless, the original name has continued to be used. The picture also had to be restored in 1975 after it was slashed by a crazed visitor, and more recently in 1990 when a viewer tossed acid on the canvas.

There is much more in the Rijksmuseum: among the superb collection of over 3,000 paintings are jewel-like vignettes by Jan Vermeer, landscapes by Ruysdael and Hobbema, pastorals by Paulus Potter, boisterous domestic scenes by Jan Steen, vigorous portraits by Frans Hals, cool interiors by Pieter de Hoogh, peasant scenes by Van Ostade. Allow at least two hours just to sample these riches, then relax in the pleasant restaurant for a snack, before going on to see the 50-odd galleries containing the magnificent collection of furniture, glass, porcelain, gold and silver. A new wing adds art and artifacts from pre-history to 1900. There is also an Asiatic department in the basement.

A few blocks down the road is the Rijksmuseum Vincent van Gogh, the only museum in Holland devoted to a single artist. The largest collection of works by van Gogh in the world, the museum contains 500 paintings and 200 drawings by the artist, as well as works by some 50 other painters of the period.

Next door is the Stedelijk Museum (Municipal Museum), its austere neoclassical facade designed to counterbalance the Rijksmuseum's neo-Gothic turrets. The museum has a stimulating collection of modern art and ever-changing displays of contemporary art. Before viewing the works of Cézanne, Chagall, Kandinsky, and Mondriaan, check the list of temporary exhibitions in Room 1. Museum policy is to trace the development of an artist rather than merely to show a few masterpieces. There is also a lovely restaurant, which overlooks the modern sculpture garden.

Diagonally opposite the Stedelijk Museum at the end of the broad Museumplein is the Concertgebouw, which presents a full and varied schedule by the Royal Concertgebouworkest along with many visiting orchestras. The building has two auditoria, the smaller one being used for chamber music and recitals. A block or two to the west of the Concert Hall is Vondelpark, an elongated rectangle of paths, lakes and pleasant shady trees. A monument honors the 17th-century epic poet Vondel, after whom the park is named. During the summer, a full schedule of free concerts and plays are performed in the park.

While you are exploring Amsterdam, keep one ear cocked for the unmistakable strains of a street organ. These remarkable instruments pour forth a torrent of sound generated by a bizarre mixture of drums, pipes, and cymbals.

One old part of Amsterdam that must be mentioned and is certainly worth exploring is the Jordaan, the area between Prinsengracht and Lijnsbaansgracht and Rozengracht and Brouwersgracht. The canals and side streets in this part all have the names of flowers and plants. Indeed at one time, when this was the French quarter of the city, the area was known as *le jardin,* a name that over the years has become Jordaan. The best time to explore the old town is on a Sunday morning when there are not too many cars and people about, or for an evening stroll. The area is attracting a lot of artists and is becoming a trendy "Bohemian" quarter, with small restaurants, antique shops, boutiques, and galleries.

The Outskirts of Amsterdam

On the southern edge of the city is the Olympic stadium, completed for the Olympic Games in 1928 and accommodating 80,000 spectators. Close by is the Haarlemmermeer Station, site of the Electrische Museumtramlijn Amsterdam (City Tram Museum). This is one of the very best spots in town for children. Take a ride on one of the old trams (summer weekends only) to the Amsterdam woods, where, incidentally, a short walk takes you to the delightful old farm house of Meerzicht.

Just beyond the stadium is one of Amsterdam's proudest achievements: the Bosplan or Forest Park, stretching for several miles, almost to Schiphol Airport. As large as Paris' Bois de Boulogne, twice as big as New York's Central Park, it was started in 1934 as a relief project during the Depression. Its more than 2,200 acres is about half woodland and includes mile after mile of bicycle paths, bridle paths, footpaths, and roadways plus an open-air theater, a score of soccer fields, a rowing course 733 meters (2,400 yards) long, a lake with paddleboats, and many other sports facilities. The land used for this far-reaching development has been reclaimed at the cost of constructing a 322 kilometer (200-mile) network of drainage pipes. In the past four decades the park has been colonized by birds and other wildlife.

Nearer to Schiphol Airport is Europe's largest artificial ski slope. Called the Meerberg, it's near the Golden Tulip Schiphol Hotel in Hoofddorp.

A visit to the Amstelpark with its modern sculptures, restaurant, sauna and rose exhibition, is a pleasant way to spend an afternoon.

Despite some complaints that the city is overpriced, overcrowded and over-rated, Amsterdam remains one of Europe's less expensive and most charming towns. The Dutch take care to preserve their architecture as well as carrying out innovative expansion schemes stretching out into the surrounding countryside. Some fine examples of continental city-planning and urbanization are to be seen, especially towards the Schiphol area, all of them characterized by the Dutch love of greenery, flowers, parks and decorative waters. There is actually an underground metro whose construction was no small job in sandy soil below sea level.

Call in at the VVV in front of Central Station to get particulars of sight-seeing excursions in and around Amsterdam and make hotel or theater reservations.

PRACTICAL INFORMATION FOR AMSTERDAM

GETTING TO TOWN FROM THE AIRPORT. The best way to reach the center of Amsterdam from Schiphol Airport is by using the new direct rail link, with three stops en route to Central Station. This runs every 10 to 15 minutes throughout the day and takes roughly half an hour to Amsterdam Central Station. Fare, second class, is Fl. 4.

Taxis, readily available, are expensive, costing from around Fl. 50. KLM bus services run a shuttle service between the airport and most Deluxe hotels, twice hourly.

TELEPHONE CODES. The telephone code for Amsterdam is 020. When dialing from within the city, no prefix is required.

HOTELS. Amsterdam is a pedestrian's paradise but a driver's nightmare. Few hotels have parking lots, and cars are best abandoned in one of the city's multi-story lots for the duration of your stay. Most visitors prefer to stay inside the concentric ring of canals that surround the downtown area. Within this, the quiet museum quarter is a convenient choice, close to both the Rijksmuseum and Vondelpark. More atmospheric is the historic canalside neighborhood with its gabled merchants' houses. At Easter and in the peak summer months (mid-June to September) they fill to bursting, and advance reservations are essential. The VVV accommodations office outside the Central Station can usually find a room for you, however, if you arrive without a booking.

We have divided the hotels in our listings into four categories—Deluxe, Expensive, Moderate and Inexpensive. In *Deluxe* hotels, two people in a double room can expect to pay from Fl. 450 to 600, in *Expensive* hotels from Fl. 300 to 450, in *Moderate* hotels from Fl. 200 to 300 and in *Inexpensive* hotels from under Fl. 200. These prices include service charge, VAT and, for the cheaper grades, usually breakfast as well. Most hotels, particularly at the upper end of the scale, have rooms in more than one price category. Be very sure to check *before* making your reservations what category of room you are booking. Deluxe and Expensive hotels all have bathrooms in the rooms; in the lower grades bathrooms are usually down the corridor, but they will always be spotlessly clean.

Prices for single rooms are around 80% of double room costs.

Deluxe

American. 79 Leidsekade; 624–5322. 185 rooms with bath. The Art Deco coffee shop, which is a protected monument, is a popular gathering place for artists and performers. The hotel is in the heart of the city, close to major theaters and restaurants.

Amstel Inter-Continental. 1 Prof. Tulpplein; 622–6060. The grand old lady of Amsterdam hotels opened in 1879, has had a year-long face-lift. With reopening slated for early 1992, it will have 60 junior suites, 18 (2- or 3-room) executive suites, a king-size royal suite, riverside restaurant, full fitness center with indoor pool, and classically elegant meeting rooms to rank among the premier hostelries in the Dutch capital. The service is likewise expected to remain exquisite.

Amsterdam Hilton. 138 Apollolaan; 678–0780 or 800–HILTONS in U.S. 276 rooms with bath. The lobby has a fireplace, and the open terrace is on one of Amsterdam's prettiest canals. The *Terrace* restaurant, *Half Moon Bar,* and an excellent, if expensive, Japanese restaurant complete the hotel's amenities.

Apollo. 2 Apollolaan (main entrance on Stadionweg); 673–5922. At the junction of five canals, this Trust House Forte hotel has 225 rooms with bath, plus a fine restaurant, private dock, and a large parking lot. (Do not confuse it with the less pretentious Apollofirst close by.)

De l'Europe. 2–4 Nieuwe Doelenstraat; 623–4836. 100 rooms with bath. This hotel hides modern amenities behind a Victorian facade. It has larger than average rooms, which are often decorated with old prints and Empire furniture. Apart from its internationally renowned *Excelsior* restaurant and a terrace overlooking the Amstel, the de l'Europe has a sophisticated leisure complex with a swimming pool in the style of a Roman spa.

Golden Tulip Barbizon. 7 Stadhouderskade; 685–1351. Near Vondel Park and Leidseplein, ten minutes from the Dam. 240 rooms with bath.

Golden Tulip Barbizon Palace. 59–72 Prins Hendrikkade; 556–4564. 226 rooms with bath. Incorporating 15 historic buildings, this hotel was built on one of the oldest developed sites in Amsterdam. Gourmet restaurant; fitness center.

Golden Tulip Pulitzer. 315–331 Prinsengracht; 523–5235. 250 rooms with bath. One of Europe's most ambitious restorations, using the shells of a row of 17th-century canalside houses, was carried out on this hotel. The refined atmosphere is sustained by a modern art gallery, oak beams, and "no two alike" split-level rooms. The management tries to provide regular guests with their favorite rooms.

Grand Hotel Krasnapolsky. 9 Dam; 554–9111. 330 rooms, all with bath. The splendid *Winter Garden* restaurant here has been restored to its turn-of-the-century grandeur. An eclectic interior embraces Victoriana and Art Deco. Other amenities are Japanese and French restaurants and fitness and business centers.

Holiday Inn Crown Plaza. 5 Nieuwe Zijds Voorburgwal; 620–0500 or 800–465–4329 in U.S. This newish chain hotel has large rooms (86 rooms, 5 suites), well-equipped baths, and individual air-conditioning. The decor is modern, with bright colors, lots of light and glass. Also featured are an indoor patio bar, coffee shop and restaurant, plus the best fitness center in town.

Marriott. 19–21 Stadhouderskade; 683–5151 or 800–228–9290 in U.S. 395 rooms, 3 suites. This huge, busy, commercial, and friendly hotel has large, redecorated guest rooms in striking new colors; the American-style bathrooms are a treat. The hotel, which is across from the Leidseplein and the new casino, also has the *Library Bar,* two restaurants, and a shopping arcade.

Okura Intercontinental. 333 Ferd. Bolstraat; 678–7111 or 800–421–0000 in U.S. 402 rooms with bath, 20 suites, studios, and Japanese-style rooms. The rooftop *Le Ciel Bleu* has French cuisine and splendid views; two ground floor restaurants serve the best Japanese food in Holland. Parking garage.

SAS Royal. 11–13 Rusland; 627–6921. This high-tech hotel has an atrium with a waterfall, 235 rooms, and seven suites with Scandinavian, Dutch, and Japanese decor. Full five-star service, with emphasis on personal attention.

Schiphol Hilton. Herbergierstraat, Schiphol Centrum; 603–4567 or 800–HILTONS in U.S. 275 rooms. Two minutes from Schiphol Airport by courtesy bus, this inn is a pleasant hub for people on the go. Locals come from the city center to use the attractive lobby bar.

Sonesta, 1 Kattengat; 621–2223 or 800–SONESTA in U.S. 425 rooms, all with bath. Near the old port area, this U.S.-style hotel has a restaurant, fitness club, shopping arcade, and a huge collection of modern art. Sunday morning coffee concerts are held in the adjacent copper-domed former church, which is now the hotel's conference center (linked by an underground passage).

Expensive

Caransa Crest. 19 Rembrandtsplein; 622–9455. 70 rooms with bath. This hotel is in the middle of a busy nightlife district, near the Music Theater, and has a restaurant.

Doelen Crest. 24 Nieuwe Doelenstraat; 622–0722. 86 rooms, most with bath. Traditional, old-fashioned comfort is available here. Ask for a room on the quieter canal side. Excellent restaurant and bar.

Golden Tulip Barbizon Schiphol. 495 Kruisweg, Hoofddorp; 020–655–0550. 244 recently redecorated rooms. Close to airport with free shuttle-bus service every 30 minutes. No charge for children (through age 16) sharing adults' room. Pets welcome.

Holiday Inn. 2 de Boelelaan; 426–2300 or 800–465–4339 in U.S. 263 rooms with bath or shower, penthouse suites. *Bourgogne* restaurant, coffee shop, bar.

Ladbroke Park. 25 Stadhouderskade; 671–7474. 183 rooms, most with bath. A step away from the Rijksmuseum and next door to the Vondel-park.

Scandic Crown Victoria. 1–6 Damrak, opposite the station; 623–4255. 150 rooms, all with bath or shower. This recently renovated and distinguished older hotel has a central location.

Schiller Crest. 26 Rembrandtsplein; 623–1660. 86 rooms with bath. The Schiller is central, with a popular sidewalk cafe and restaurant.

Moderate

Acca. 3a Van de Veldestraat; 662–5262. This well-appointed small hotel is near the Museumplein.

Ambassade. 341 Herengracht; 626–2333. 27 rooms, all with bath. With its canalside location, Louis XV decor, and Oriental carpets, the Ambassade seems more like a stately home than a hotel. Gracious service.

Cok First Class Hotel. 34–36 Koninginneweg; 664–6111. 40 comfortable rooms overlooking Vondel Park, good restaurant. There are also two adjoining hotels in the lower price range (**Cok Tourist/Cok Budget**).

Jan Luyken. Jan Luykenstraat 54–58; 676–4111. Two buildings offer 63 charming guest rooms with modern furnishings and some garden views. A bar-coffee shop-lounge serves soups and snacks 1 P.M.–1 A.M. There is no air-conditioning, but the hotel's excellent location in the museum area, traditional charm, and attentive service are desirable points.

Novotel. 10 Europaboulevard; 541–1123. 600 rooms and several restaurants. This, mammoth hotel, is big, modern, and somewhat anonymous.

Die Port van Cleve. 178 N.Z. Voorburgwal; 624–4860. 110 rooms with bath. Though central, this hotel breathes antiquity and quietness.

Pullman Schiphol. 20 Oude Haagseweg; 617–9005. On the main road to Den Haag. 158 rooms with shower. Restaurant. Good service.

Rembrandt Crest. 255 Herengracht; 622–1727. 110 rooms with bath. This attractive hotel is on the elegant Gentlemen's Canal.

De Roode Leeuw. 93 Damrak; 624–0396. 80 rooms, newly renovated. Pleasant sidewalk terrace. Traditional Dutch food. Around the corner from the Dam.

Sander. 69 Jac. Obrechtstraat; 662–7574. Family atmosphere, excellent service. Wide price range. Closed Jan. and Feb.

Trianon. 3 J.W. Brouwerstraat; 673–2073 or 800–528–1234 in U.S. 58 rooms. A Best Western Hotel, next to the concert hall and close to all major museums.

Inexpensive

Agora. 462 Singel; 627–2200. Set beside the Singel flower market, this small hotel has light and spacious rooms, some decorated with period furnishings. The recently refurbished 18th-century house has a summery dining room. Considerate staff and a relaxed neighborhood.

Casa 400. 75 James Wattstraat; 665–1171. 400 rooms with shower. All the amenities—American bar, two restaurants, sun lounges, plus a nursery for the kids. Closed Oct.–May.

Hans Brinker Student Class Hotel. 136–138 Kerkstraat; 622–0687. 52 rooms; restaurants and bars. A student budget hotel with doubles and dormitory-style rooms.

Het Canal House. 148 Keizersgracht; 622–5182. 26 spacious rooms overlook the canal or the illuminated garden. This canalside hotel puts antiques instead of TVs in the rooms, but it does have a newly installed elevator. The American owners greet new guests personally to offer tips about Amsterdam.

Kap. 5b Den Texstraat; 624–5908. 35 rooms. This pleasant place is family-run.

Museumzicht. 22 Jan Luykenstraat; 671–2954. 27 rooms, few with bath.

Slotania. 133 Slotermeerlaan; 613–4568. A bit far from the center, but accessible via good connections on city transport. Pleasant restaurant.

Wiechmann. 328–330 Prinsengracht; 626–3321 or 622–5410. 35 rooms, some with bath. Situated on the edge of the lively Jordaan, this hotel is popular for quiet warmth and reasonable prices. Bedrooms are modern but modest. Book out of season or well in advance.

Zandbergen. 205 Willemsparkweg; 676–9321. This small 18-room establishment overlooking the park has very well-equipped rooms; convenient to museums and concert hall. Breakfast included.

Youth Hostels. There are a number of youth hostels in Amsterdam offering accommodations from Fl. 20 to Fl. 35 per night, including breakfast. Full details are available from Stichting Nederlandse Jeugdherberg Centrale, 4 Prof. Tulpplein, Amsterdam (tel. 551–3133); or from the VVV at the Central Station. Two of the best are *Stadsdoelen,* 97 Kloveniersburgwal; 624–6832, and *Vondelpark,* 5 Zandpad; 683–1744

Camping. There are two large campsites in the Amsterdam area. The first is at 45 Ijsbaanpad (tel. 662–0916), the other, **Het Amsterdamse Bos,** at 1 Kleine Noorddijk, Aalsmeer (tel. 641–6868). They are open from April to October but can get very full in high season, so book ahead. Write to the VVV for their *Camping* brochure.

GETTING AROUND. By Bus, Tram and Metro. Armed with a route map, available from the VVV, you should have no trouble getting around. A zonal fare system is used, with metro tickets purchased from automatic dispensers, tram and bus tickets from drivers (all of whom speak English!). One of the most useful tickets is the *Strippenkaart* (strip ticket) from which bits are stamped as they are used up, according to the number of zones crossed. Don't forget that more than one person can travel on a *Strippenkaart,* it just gets used up more quickly! If you are going to travel about a lot in Amsterdam, buy one of the runabout tickets, *Dagkaart.* These are available for 1 day (Fl. 9.50), 2 days (Fl. 12.60), 3 days (Fl. 15.60) and 4 days (Fl. 18.50). Buy them from the bus or tram driver, at Central Station, Amstel Station, or at 15 Leidseplein. Please note that at the time of writing (mid-1991), price rises were imminent; contact the train station for details at tel. 627–2727.

If your travels are taking you throughout Holland, don't forget the public transport Link Passes which can be added onto the NS Rail Passes.

By Taxi. Taxis are expensive. Pick-up charge is Fl. 4, and charges thereafter are Fl. 2 to Fl. 4 per kilometer. Taxis are not usually hailed in the

street, but taken from ranks, normally near stations, or at key road inter-
sections. To call a taxi, dial 677–7777. Water taxis are also available. The
rates are similar to those for normal taxis, but Fl. 2 *per minute* instead
of per kilometer; tel. 622–2181.

On Foot/By Bicycle. Amsterdam is a small congested city full of narrow streets—ideal for exploring on foot. But be sure to get a good map,
available from the VVV. Bicycles are available for hire for around Fl. 7.50
per day. They are perhaps the easiest way to get around, but be careful
of the traffic. A high deposit is payable, usually Fl. 100 to Fl. 200. Details
available from the VVV—request their seven excellent brochures on unusual walking tours. Ask about Ena's Bike Tour, a 7½ hour escorted trip
to the Vinkeveense Lake, costing Fl. 37.50 (tel. 015–143797). The Yellow
Bike Tours (tel. 620–6940) organizes city tours by bike or on foot, as well
as longer bike tours through the countryside to local fishing villages (Apr.–
Oct.).

Canal and City Tours. Perhaps the best and most enjoyable introduction
to Amsterdam is a boat trip along the canals. Several operators run trips,
usually in glass-roofed boats. There are frequent departures from starting
points opposite the Central Station, by Smits Koffiehuis, beside the Dam-
rack, along the Rokin and Stadhouderskade (near the Rijksmuseum) and
from several other spots. Most trips have multilingual guides, and last
from 1 to 1½ hours. They cost from Fl. 9 to Fl. 15. Most also take in the
busy harbor. A few have facilities for wheelchairs.

Even more delightful are the night-time trips that run in the summer.
They are more expensive (Fl. 35) but wine and cheese are usually included
in the price, and in any case the sight of the city's graceful and dignified
17th-century mansions slipping by in the twilight, their lights glistening
in the water, should not be missed. Dinner cruises are also available, from
a cold buffet to a five-course gourmet dinner. (Call Rederij Lovers, tel.
622–2181; and Holland International, 626–2448). You can also now hire
pedal-boats to make your own canal tours. Called Canal-Bike, they cost
Fl. 18 per hour; slightly more if they provide wine and cheese in the evening. For details call 626–5574. Ask the VVV for their *Cruises in Amsterdam* brochure.

Bus tours around the city are also available and provide a reasonable
introduction to Amsterdam. Price is from Fl. 30, duration around 3 hours.
Most of these trips include a brief visit to the Rijksmuseum and to a dia-
mond-cutting factory. Tours on Sundays also include a canal trip.

TOURIST INFORMATION. The main tourist information office (VVV)
is at the Central Station (tel. 020–626–6444). It is open every day Easter–
Sept. from 9 A.M. to 11 P.M.; Oct.–Easter Mon.–Fri. 9–6, Sat. 9–5, Sun. 10–
1, 2–5. The office has an accommodations service for those who arrive
without reservations; a small fee is charged for this. They can also make
theater and excursion bookings (including canal trips) as well as supplying
maps, restaurant lists, sightseeing checklists etc. There is always at least
one person on duty who speaks English. There is another VVV office at
106 Leidsestraat (closed Sun.).

USEFUL ADDRESSES. Travel Agents. *American Express,* 66 Damrak
(tel. 626–2042). *Key Tours* (*Wagonlits Cooks*), 19 Dam (tel. 624–7310),
and at Amstel Hotel, 1 Prof. Tulpplein (tel. 622–6060). Holland Interna-

tional, 54 Rokin and elsewhere (tel. 551–2812/622–2550/673–0868). *Lindbergh,* 26 Damrak (tel. 622–2766).

Consulates. *American Consulate,* 19 Museumplein (tel. 679–0321). *British Consulate,* 44 Koningslaan (tel. 676–4343).

Car Hire. *Adam's Rent-a-Car,* 344–347 Nassaukade (tel. 685–0111). *Avis-Rent-a-Car,* 380 Nassaukade (tel. 683–6061). *Hertz,* 333 Overtoom (tel. 685–2441). *Europcar,* 51–53 Overtoom (tel. 683–2123). *Budget,* 121 Overtoom (tel. 612–6066).

All the leading car-hire companies have desks at Schiphol Airport.

MUSEUMS. Amsterdam has over 40 museums, ranging from the quaint and local to the internationally renowned. For the really serious museum-buff, the Museum Ticket (*Museumkaart*) will get you into 16 museums in Amsterdam (and about 350 more all over the country). Issued by VVV offices, it costs Fl. 15 for those under 25, Fl. 40 for those 25 and over, and Fl. 25 for senior citizens. Note that most museums close on Mondays. April–Sept. there is a special "Museum Boat," a shuttle boat visiting 11 of the city's most famous museums at six stops (tel. 622–2181). Cost is Fl. 12, valid all day and including some discounts on admissions.

Allard Pierson Museum. 127 Oude Turfmarkt. Archeological finds from Mesopotamia, Egypt, Greece, Italy. Open 10–5, Tues.–Fri., 1–5 Sat. and Sun. Closed Mon. Adm. Fl. 3.

Amsterdams Historisch Museum (Historical Museum). 92 Kalverstraat. Housed in a renovated orphanage. Good depiction of the city from earliest times. Interesting coffee and diamond trade exhibits; fascinating collection of jewelry. Fairly good restaurant. Open daily 11–5. Adm. Fl. 5.

Anne Frank Huis (Anne Frank Museum). 263 Prinsengracht. The house in which the young Jewish girl Anne Frank, author of the famous diary, hid from the Nazis during World War II. The rooms where the family was hidden are open to visitors and there are other moving wartime exhibits. Open 9–5, Mon.–Sat., 10–5 Sun. (until 7 in summer). Adm. Fl. 6.

Aviodome National Lucht- en Ruimtevaartmuseum (Aviodome National Aeronautical Museum). Schiphol. Exhibition of aviation and space travel, past and present, with a glimpse into the future. Also includes the recently opened information center that concentrates on Schiphol's plans for expansion. Open May–Sept. daily 10–5; from Oct.–Apr. 10–5, Tues.–Fri., 12–5 Sat. and Sun. Adm. Fl. 7.

Begijnhof. Entrance on Spui. A haven of rest with two churches and a cluster of 17th-century homes around a garden of flowers, dating back to 1346.

Bijbels Museum (Bible Museum). 366 Herengracht. Biblical antiquities from Palestine, Egypt and Mesopotamia, Open 10–5, Tues.–Sat., 1–5 Sun. Closed Mon. Adm. Fl. 4.

Electrische Museumtramlijn Amsterdam (Amsterdam Tram Museum). 264 Amstelveenseweg. In the old Haarlemmermeer Station. Includes weekend rides on old city trams. Open Apr.–Oct. 1–4 Tues.–Thurs. and Sat., 10.30–5.30 Sun.; Closed Nov.–Mar. Adm. Fl. 3.

Joods Historisch Museum. 2–4 Jonas Daniel Meijerplein. Jewish historical museum housed in three former synagogues. Open daily 11–5. Adm. Fl. 8.

Katten Kabinet (Cat Museum). 497 Herengracht. Amsterdam's newest museum is devoted to famous felines. Open Tues.–Sun. 12–5. Adm. Fl. 7.

Madame Tussaud. 20 Dam Square. Tells the story of Dutch people and events through the ages in life-size wax models. Open daily from 10–6, in summer 9–7 Adm. Fl. 8.

Museum Amstelkring Ons' Lieve Heer op Solder (Our Lord in the Attic). 40 Oudezijds Voorburgwal. From the outside this is a typical 17th-century merchant's home (in the red light district). On the top floor, however, is a remarkable attic Catholic church that dates from the Reformation when non-Protestants were forbidden to worship. Open Mon.–Sat., 10–5, Sun. 1–5. Adm. Fl. 4.

Museum Het Rembranthuis (Rembrandt Museum). 4–6 Jodenbreestraat. Dating from 1606 this fascinating house was the home of the painter from 1639–1658. Open Mon.–Sat. 10–5, Sun. and holidays 1–5. Adm. Fl. 5.

Nederlands Filmmuseum. 3 Vondelpark. Film reviews, photographs, playbills, shows; library; changing exhibitions. Open Tues.–Sat. 11–5. Adm. Fl. 2.

Nederlands Scheepvaart Museum (Maritime Museum). 1 Kattenburgerplein. Historical ship models, paintings, prints, maps, nautical instruments, and ships from yesteryear at dockside. Open 10–5, Tues.–Sat., 1–5 Sun. Closed Mon. Adm. Fl. 6.

NINT, Nederlands Instituut voor Nijverheid en Techniek (Dutch Institute for Industry and Technology). 129 Tolstraat. Brand-new hands-on exhibits relating to natural science and especially technology. Open Mon.–Fri. 10–5, Sat. and Sun. 1–5. Closed public holidays. Adm. Fl. 6.

Rijksmuseum. 42 Stadhouderskade. A vast Victorian red-brick building facing the outermost of the city's concentric ring of canals and the country's most prestigious and important museum. Superb collection of Dutch 16th- and 17th-century paintings, plus magnificent Flemish, Italian and Spanish works. Apart from the Rembrandts, it is worth searching out Jan Steen's family portraits; Frans Hals's drunken scenes; van Ruysdael's romantic but menacing landscapes; and Vermeer's glimpses of everyday life bathed in pale light. Useful cafeteria available. Conducted tours at 11 and 2.30. Open 10–5, Tues–Sat., 1–5 Sun. Closed Mon. Adm. Fl. 8.

Rijksmuseum Vincent van Gogh. 7 Paulus Potterstraat. Unrivaled collection of 500 paintings and 200 drawings by the artist, along with library and many other documents. *The Potato Eaters,* one of two paintings stolen from here, was returned in April 1989, but the other remains missing. Attractive cafeteria with terrace in summer. Open 10–5, Tues.–Sat., 1–5 Sun. Closed Mon. Adm. Fl. 8.

Six Collection. 218 Amstel. Home of the descendants of Jan Six. Ten generations ago Jan Six was, among other things, a patron and friend of Rembrandt, who painted his portrait, which still hangs here. A guided tour is normally at 11 A.M. (Write in advance to Jan Six, 218 Amstel, 1017 AJ Amsterdam, NL.)

Stedelijk Museum (Municipal Museum). 13 Paulus Potterstraat. Excellent collections of modern art, plus good late 19th- and early 20th-century works. Open daily 11–5. Adm. Fl. 8.

Theater Instituut. 168 Herengracht. Set in two frescoed Louis XIV-style houses, the museum documents history of the Dutch theater through prints, drawings, costumes, programs, and videos of stage productions. Changing exhibitions. In summer, the large garden is open for buffet lunches. Open 11–5, Tues.–Sun. Closed Mon. Adm. Fl. 3.

Tropenmuseum (Tropical Museum). 2 Linnaeusstraat. Exhibits on all aspects of the Third World. Open 10–5, Mon.–Fri., 12–5 Sat. and Sun. Adm. Fl. 5.

Van Loonmuseum, 672 Keizersgracht. This 17th-century canalside house is furnished in magnificent period style. Open Mon. 10–5 only.

Willet Holthuysen Museum. 605 Herengracht. Characteristic and delightful 17th-century merchant's mansion. Open Tues.–Sun. 11–5. Adm. Fl. 2.50.

CHURCHES. Begijnhof Both the Protestant and Catholic churches here have fascinating histories. **Nieuw Kerk** This church, café and exhibition center is open Mon.–Sun. 11–5 (closed Jan. and Feb.) **Oude Kerk.** In summer, the church is open Mon.–Sat. 11–5, closes two hours earlier in winter. The tower is open June–Sept. Mon. and Thurs. 2–5, Tues. and Wed. 11–3. Admission to the carillon concerts is Fl. 8. **Portuguese Synagogue.** Open Sun–Fri. 10–12:15 and 1:30–4 **Westerkerk.** Open 15 May–15 Sept. Mon.–Sat. 10–4. The view from the steeple is fabulous. It can be visited June through Sept., Tues.–Sat. 2–5.

BOTANICAL GARDENS, ZOO, AND AQUARIUM. These three make up a large complex just to the east of the downtown area along the Plantage Kerklaan. Coming from the downtown area, you first reach the *Hortus Botanicus* (Botanical Gardens), with hothouses and nurseries and plants galore (2 Middenlaan. Open Apr.–Oct. Mon.–Fri. 9–5, Sat. and Sun. 11–5; in the winter open until 4 P.M.) A block further along is the *Natura Artis Magistra* (better known as the Zoo) at 40 Plantage Kerklaan, with everything from insects to elephants. Open daily 9–5. Finally, there is the Aquarium (in the Zoo), a characteristic representative of the species; one of the highlights here is the electric eels who are periodically stimulated into lighting up a row of bulbs. A recent addition to the complex is a newly-built Planetarium, the country's largest, which offers a variety of presentations.

ENTERTAINMENT. Music and Concerts. In the music department, Amsterdam's famous Royal Concertgebouw Orchestra ranks among the foremost in Europe. It plays in the Concertgebouw, 2–6 Concertgebouwplein (tel. 671–8345). The box office is open 10–4 for personal callers, 10–3 for telephone bookings. Wednesday lunchtime concerts are free. Entertainment can also be booked at the Amsterdam Uit Buro, near the Stadsschouwburg, 26 Leidseplein; 621–1211. The same building has a smaller auditorium that is used for chamber music, recitals and even jam sessions. For opera and ballet, the national companies are housed in the new Muziektheater at 1 Amstel. During the Holland Festival foreign companies also perform. For information on the annual Holland Festival contact— Holland Festival, 21 Kleine Gartmanplantsoen, 1017 PK Amsterdam (tel. 627–6566). The Stalhouderij Theatre, 1e Bloemdwarsstraat 4 (tel. 646–2282) has an international cast which has gained wide acclaim. It is hoping to move to larger quarters soon. Until then, its productions are scheduled in various locations, so phone ahead for information. The former Shaffy

Theater, Keizersgracht 324, now renamed the Felix Maritis (tel. 623–1311) performs plays (usually in Dutch), cabarets and unconventional shows.

For details of current performances—including rock and jazz—see the *Amsterdam Times* and *Amsterdam This Week*, monthly and weekly listings of events and entertainments available from the VVV. The VVV can also make bookings for most performances.

Movie theaters are scattered throughout Amsterdam, the biggest concentrations being on Leidseplein and Reguliersbreestraat. Performances begin at fixed hours, often 1.30, 3.45, 6.45 and 9.30 P.M. Smoking is forbidden in all theaters and movie houses. Sound tracks are usually in the original language with Dutch subtitles, but some are dubbed, so check first. To see what's playing when and where, see *Amsterdam This Week*.

ALTERNATIVE AMSTERDAM. Paradiso, in a converted church, is still famous from the drug days of the '60s and the provo's (kabouters), is at 6–8 Weteringschans (tel. 626–4521). Now has pop concerts, classical music, cinema, workshops, jazz, reading table, café, macrobiotic restaurant, etc. Open Tues.–Sat., 8–1 A.M., Fri., Sat. 8–2 A.M.

Akhnaton, Bakhorst 12 (tel. 624–3396), a youth center for young working people as well as students, with performances of theater, concerts, films.

Korsakov. 161 Lijnbaansgracht. An eclectic bar-disco run by ex-squatters. Best at weekends.

Kosmos, 142 Prins Hendrikkade. Meditation center including yoga, zen, astrology, alternative medicine, herbs, food, film, theater, lectures, café, macrobiotic restaurant and even a sauna.

Melkweg (Milky Way), 234a Lijnbaansgracht, (tel. 626–7477), behind the main city theater. A multi-media center with film, theater, video, pop, jazz, poetry, mime, jam sessions, tea rooms with a sweet heady scent in the air, art market, etc. There are weekend club nights with a number of African and other ethnic bands performing.

SHOPPING. Amsterdam's chief shopping streets, which have largely been turned into pedestrian-only areas, are the youth-oriented Kalverstraat and Nieuwendijk (on opposite sides of the Dam); the somber and sedate Rokin, where some of the best antiques dealers are found (the rest of their colleagues are in the area of the Spiegelgracht, Nieuwe Spiegelstraat, Kerkstraat); and the more up-market Leidsestraat, P.C. Hooftstraat, Van Baerlestraat, and Beethovenstraat. The last three feature couture clothing and fine housewares. Ask for the city's four shopping guides on markets, department stores, chic fashion, crafts, art, and antiques; all available from the VVV (Fl. 10).

Tax Rebates of 15.5% on sales tax are available to all visitors from non-EC countries for purchases, made in one store, costing over $150 (Fl. 300). Ask the shop where you made the purchase for your tax rebate check (and a BTW 0B90 certificate). You can collect refunds by mail or from "cash points" at Schiphol Airport or main border crossings.

Markets

There's a lively flea market on the Waterlooplein around the Muziektheater (weekdays only, 11–4). The flower market is held on the Singel Mon.–

Sat.; a colorful and vivid experience. Noisier, is the bird market held every Saturday in the Noordmarkt. On Monday morning, Noordmarkt is a general market. The more studious might be interested in the stamp market, Wed. and Sat. afternoon, at Nieuwezijds Voorburgwal and the book market at Oudemanhuispoort, held Mon.–Sat. Art Markets are held on Thorbeckeplein and at the Spui, from Apr. through Oct. every Sun. 12–6. But the best general market is at Albert Cuypstraat, held all day Mon.–Sat.

Diamonds

Moving upmarket rather sharply, no visit to Amsterdam is complete without a visit to one of the major cutting houses. Apart from the fascination of watching the cutting, there is usually no pressure to buy. A lucky thing, too—diamonds may be forever, but they are also terribly expensive!

Among the leading cutting houses are:

Amsterdam Diamond Center B.V., 1–5 Rokin (tel. 624–5787); *Coster Diamonds,* 2–4 Paulus Potterstraat (tel. 676–2222); *Gassan Diamonds,* 173–175 Nieuwe Uilenburgerstraat (tel. 622–5333); *Holshuysen - Stoeltie B.V.,* 13–17 Wagenstraat (tel. 623–7601); *A. Van Moppes & Zoon B.V.,* 2–6 Albert Cuypstraat (tel. 676–1242).

Most are open daily 9–5, and all will be glad to show you around.

Antiques

Amsterdam is one of Europe's leading centers for antiques, from every source, of every type, from every age. The area around Nieuwe Spiegelstraat is full of small antique shops, specialized and general. The Joordan district also has many shops. In addition, there are several important antique markets held each week, featuring stalls for everything from the worthless to the, perhaps, priceless. As well as the flea market on Waterlooplein, other antique markets include: Antiekmarkt de Looier, 109 Elandsgracht, open Mon.–Thurs. 11–5, Sat. 9–5 (tel. 264–9038); De Eland, 68 Elandsgracht (tel. 623–0343); and De Zwan, 474 Keizersgracht (tel. 624–7601). The famous Christie's, 57 Cornelius Schuytstraat (tel. 664–2011), and Sotheby's, 102 Rokin (tel. 627–5656), have monthly auctions, with viewing days beforehand. During the summer, some of these auctions are held on Sundays. From May to September, an antiques fair is also held on Sundays in the vicinity of the Music Theater and is particularly good for silver and toys. In *Amsterdam Antiques,* 34 Nieuwe Spiegelstraat (tel. 625–3371), 12 dealers are gathered under one roof. The range covers Spanish armor, Russian icons and old dolls.

Porcelain

Fine porcelain, particularly imported Wedgwood, is obtainable at *Van Gelder & Co.,* J. Rebelstraat (closed Saturdays), or in their narrow branch store at Van Baerlestraat 40 (tel. 662–0668). A wide range of Delftware is also to be seen at Focke and Melzer, 124 Rokin (tel. 623–1944) 65 P.C. Hoofstraat, or Okura Hotel shopping arcade.

Books

Book shops have a very large selection of new editions, second-hand books and even collectors' items in many languages, and so are often worth browsing in for half an hour or so. Bargains can also often be picked up during a stroll through Oudemanhuispoort, a unique market, between Kloveniersburgwal and Oudezijds Burgwal. Don't be put off by these tongue-twisting names; they're easier to get to than pronounce. The *Atheneum Bookshop,* 14–16 Spui (tel. 623–3933), is one of the most wide-ranging and pleasant to browse around. *Allert de Lange,* 62 Damrak, opposite the Bijenkorf, has a fascinating range of maps and travel guides, many in English. *De Sleghte,* 48–52 Kalverstraat (also Coolsingel, Rotterdam) is a good place to browse. They sell foreign books as well as Dutch ones and on any topic you can think of. They also sell their own reprints of old Dutch maps, engravings and prints at reasonable prices. Also reproductions. *Antiquariaat,* 14–18 Oude Hoogstraat, for old books.

Miscellaneous

Go to *Jacob Hooy* at 12 Kloveniersburgwal (tel. 624–3041), an old-style drugstore filled with herb pots and drawers of spices in which the firm has been dealing for well over two centuries. For cheese, make for *De Franse Kaasmaker* at 192 Marnixstraat (tel. 626–2210). They sell 65 different varieties of cheese, especially French and Dutch.

Most shops have a wide range of French and other foreign clothes, while Dutch ready-to-wear fashions are good quality though more expensive than fashions in Britain or the States. For the young there are many small boutiques, including some interesting second-hand clothes-shops in the Joordan area and inexpensive new clothes in Albert Cuypstraat market.

Holland is famous for its cigars. One fascinating old shop for these is *Hajenius,* 92 Rokin, while at *Sigarenmakerij Nak,* 27 St. Pieterspoortsteeg, you can see demonstrations of making cigars by hand. Davidoff, 84 Van Baerlestraat, (tel. 671–1042), is famous for Cuban cigars. Another traditional Dutch craft, clog making, can be watched at *De Klompenboer,* 20 N.Z. Vorburgwal (tel. 623–0632).

Lazy (or tired) shoppers could do worse than call in at one of the big department stores like the *Bijenkorf,* 90A Damrak, corner Dam Square, where many name-brand fashion items are obtainable under the same roof. Although not quite so large as Macy's or Harrods, it's got just about everything, including a restaurant where the pancakes are quite delicious. Also *Vroom & Dreesmann,* 201 Kalverstraat (tel. 622–0171), near Munt Square.

RESTAURANTS. Amsterdammers are less creatures of habit than the Dutch in general. Even so, set menus and early dinners are preferred by these health-conscious citizens. For travelers on a budget (or a diet), the "Tourist Menu" sign guarantees an economical yet imaginative set menu created by the restaurant's head chef. For traditional fare, the "Nederlands Dis" soup tureen sign is a promise of regional recipes. "You can eat in any language!" is the city's proud boast, so when you're in the mood for a change from Dutch food, Indonesian, Chinese, Greek, or Turkish restaurants all offer great alternatives. Between meals, follow your nose to the nearest herring cart, or drop in on a cozy "brown café," (so-called because they are seldom decorated) for coffee and a *kroketje* (croquette). These cafés are recommended for a sample of genuine local life and food. They are a cross between a British pub and a French café and, apart from the normally exuberant atmosphere, many serve good inexpensive food.

Our restaurant lists are divided into three categories: Expensive, Moderate and Inexpensive. Per person and excluding drinks, you can expect to pay from Fl. 90 to Fl. 200 in an *Expensive* restaurant, from Fl. 50 to Fl. 100 in a *Moderate* restaurant and from Fl. 30 in an *Inexpensive* restaurant. However, these prices can be no more than approximations as most restaurants serve several dishes in more than one price category. Similarly, what you drink will affect your bill significantly. So be sure to check the menus posted outside (by law) *before* you go in. The daily *table d'hôte* set menus are best value, even in the most expensive places.

Note also that for more expensive restaurants you should book ahead. Similarly, remember that the Dutch eat early and that many restaurants are accordingly closed as early as 10 P.M. with last orders as early as 9 P.M. outside the bigger cities. Credit cards are not universally accepted, even in Expensive restaurants, so take cash along for emergencies.

Expensive

Beddington's. 8 Roolof Hartstraat; 676–5201. Served here is an unusual mix of Italian and Japanese food cooked by an English chef.

Dikker en Thijs. 444 Prinsengracht; 626–7721. Elegant second-story restaurant overlooking the canal and serving fine French cuisine; the **Café de Centre,** ground floor, for inexpensive lunches and self-service dinner.

Edo. 9 Dam, in the Grand Hotel Krasnapolsky; 554–6096. Artistically set out portions of raw fish and deep-fried *tempura* vegetables are served against a background of polished pine and equally polished service. Marvel at the way Dutch seafood lends itself to *sushi* preparation, often made at your table.

Excelsior. 2 Nieuwe Doelenstraat; 623–4836. This renowned restaurant offers a varied French menu based on local ingredients; try the seabass in curry sauce or the smoked eel. The service is discreet and impeccable.

De Kersentuin. 7 Dijsselhofplantsoen, in the Garden Hotel; 664–2121. Very modern, *nouvelle cuisine.* Highly recommended.

Prinsenkelder. 438 Prinsengracht; 626–7721. Located in a 17th-century former warehouse, this restaurant is rather formal, but features good Dutch food, with game a specialty in season, if a little expensive. Closed Mon.

Les Quatre Canetons. 111 Prinsengracht; 624–6307. Pleasantly informal, this canalside restaurant is popular with local businesspeople. It serves mainly *nouvelle cuisine* as well as young duckling; in an Oriental modern decor of neutral colors and wood tones.

Molen de Dikkert. 104a Amstelveenseweg; 741–1328. International cuisine, including Scottish beef Wellington, is served in a windmill on the outskirts of town. A favorite with business executives for lunch or dinner. Closed Sun.

La Rive. 1 Prof. Tulpplein; 622–6060. This refined riverside restaurant with an elegant English-style wood-paneled decor, graciously serves French cuisine.

Sancerre. 28 Reestraat; 622–8794. A delightful 18th-century building is home to French-Dutch cuisine. Choose from one of four menus, including an all-vegetarian one. Excellent French wines.

De Silveren Speigel. 4 Kattengat; 624–6589. Excellent French food is offered here in a charming traditional decor.

T'Brueghelhuys. 20 Smaksteeg; 624–4874. Mainly for groups, this medieval-style stop is also open for individual diners on Saturdays. Lively meals with minstrel music. Touristy place.

t' Swarte Schaep (The Black Sheep). 24 Korte Leidsedwarsstraat; 622–3021. The Black Sheep is a calm French-Dutch restaurant overlooking the frenetic Leidseplein area. In season, roast pheasant in nutmeg follows game soup or Zeeland oysters in champagne sauce. Take advantage of the set lunch for only Fl. 50. Dinner orders are accepted until 11, unusually late even for Amsterdam.

Tout Court. 13 Runstraat; 625–8637. Run by a member of the renowned Fagel family, famed for its French culinary feats. Good for after-theater parties. Closed Mon.

Trechter. 63 Hobbemakade; 671–1263. High quality *nouvelle cuisine.* Normally a waiting list for reservations. Very expensive.

d'Vijff Vlieghen (Five Flies). 269–302 Spuistraat; 624–8369. Take a trip back in time to a warren of 17th-century time. Each dining room is decorated in a different Renaissance style. Copper pots and blue Delftware cover the walls. The wild game specialties are attractive but substantial. As befits an ex-tavern, the candlelit atmosphere is warm and relaxed.

Yamazato. 333 Ferd. Bolstraat; 678–7111. Part of Okura Hotel, this is perhaps the best Japanese restaurant in town. Try the sashimi and tempura preparations. Also in the hotel is the popular *Teppan-Yaki.*

Moderate

Bali. 95 Leidsestraat; 622–7878. This is a popular Indonesian restaurant in the heart of the Leidseplein bustle. Try the *nasi goreng,* a spicy rice-based dish, or the pasta-based *bami goreng.* A vegetarian menu is also available. Since the spice sauces overshadow the taste of wine, beer or water are better accompaniments.

The Egg Creme, 19 St. Jacobstraat; 623–0575. Vegetarian meals are becoming quite popular with the Dutch. This place serves some tasty dishes in a light, pleasant atmosphere and at very reasonable prices. No alcoholic beverages.

Keijzer Bodega. 96 van Baerlestraat, next to Concertgebouw, the City Concert Hall; 671–1441. A turn-of-the-century restaurant frequented by musicians and artists. Very good food, warm atmosphere.

China Corner. On Dam Square; 622–8816 For "Dim Sum" lunch.

Claes Claez. 24 Egelantiersstraat; 625–5306. Good steaks, fish, and soups. Traditional Dutch food. Live music most nights.

Fong Lie. 80 P.C. Hoofstraat; 671–6404. Chinese food for the knowledgeable. Booking essential. Closed Mon.

De Groene Lanteerne (The Green Lantern). 43 Haarlemmerstraat near the Concertgebouw; 624–1952. Three floors high, this is the narrowest restaurant in all Holland. Crowded with bric-a-brac and atmosphere. Closed Tues.

't Heertje. 16 Herenstraat; 625–8127. Authentic Dutch dishes and ambiance. Closed Wed.

Heineken's Hoek. 1–3 Kleine Gartmanplantsoen; 623–0700. Brassy, modern café. Good for basic, moderately-priced lunches.

Mirafiori. 2 Hobbemastraat; 672–3013. Serving simple, but well-prepared Italian pastas in an attractive marble setting.

Oesterbar. 10 Leidsesplein; 623–2988. The Oyster Bar specializes in seafood, some of which eyes you fishily from tanks. The ground floor bistro offers relatively inexpensive dining, while upstairs, presentation and price are of a higher standard. Try the salmon, trout, or even the oysters.

De Orient. 21 van Baerlestraat; 673–4985. Excellent for authentic Indonesian atmosphere and cuisine.

Die Port van Cleve. 178–180 N.Z. Voorburgwal; 624–0047. Fine Dutch herring dishes in vaulted beerhall or old Dutch dining salon adorned with Delft tiles.

Rias Altao. 25 Westermarket; 624–2510. Noted for large meals, especially paella, and good house wine. One of the best Spanish restaurants in town.

De Roode Leeuw. 93–94 Damrak; 624–9683. As a "Nederlands Dis" restaurant, it guarantees traditional Dutch cuisine and varied regional dishes. Depending on the season, you can sample smoked eel, Zeeland mussels or asparagus wrapped in ham. The reasonable wine list, attentive service and friendly atmosphere live up to the "Nederland Dis" reputation.

Rose's Cantina. 38 Reguliersdwarsstraat; 625–9797. Popular and fashionable Mexican restaurant that attracts large crowds.

Sama Sebo. 27 PC Hoofstraat; 662–8146. The most varied *rijsttafel* in town.

Sea Palace. 8 Oosterdokskade; 626–4777. This is a huge, floating Chinese pavilion. The Cantonese menu is only of modest quality, but the surroundings more than make up for it. A children's menu is available.

Seoul. 106 Prins Hendrikkade; 622–3267. Good spicy Korean food.

Sluizer. 45 Utrechtsestraat; 626–3557. Two restaurants; one serving meat and the other (and better) serving fish.

Witteveen. 256 Ceintuurbaan; 662–4368. Cajun menu with blackened fish and pecan pie.

Yoichi. 128 Weteringschans; 622–6829. Excellent Japanese *sukiyaki* and *tempura* menus.

Inexpensive

Bojo. 51 Lange Leidsedwarsstraat; 622–7434. Wide range of Indonesian dishes. Crowded but open until 6 A.M.

Egg Cream. 19 Jacobstraat; 623–0575. Amsterdam's best vegetarian restaurant. with dishes that are never bland. Open 11 A.M.–8 P.M.

Haringhandel Visser. Muntplein Haringkar. Typical Dutch herring delights served from a herring cart. Closed Sun. and Mon.

Oud Holland. 105 N.Z. Voorburgwal, near the Palace; 624–6848. In a convenient location for a night on the town, and one of the few Amsterdam restaurants that offer a Tourist Menu. Typical Dutch meals include *hotchpot* (beef stew) for two and a salad.

Mouwes. 73 Utrechtsestraat; 623–5053. Excellent for kosher sandwiches and delicatessen foods. Closed Sat.

Pancake Bakery. 191 Prinsengracht; 625–1333. Pancakes for every course including dessert, for which the toppings could be ice cream, fruit or liqueur. Decorated in cluttered Dutch rustic style, the Bakery has a friendly, busy atmosphere.

Speciaal. 142 Nieuwe Leliestraat; 624–9706. Although set in the picturesque Jordaan area, this Indonesian restaurant is slightly off the beaten track and looks very unspecial from outside. Inside, however, the soothing Indonesian prints and raffiawork create an intimate effect, and the chicken, fish, and egg dishes provide tasty variants on a sweet and sour theme.

Bars

Amsterdam bars tend to be one of three types: *proeflokaal* (old tasting houses for wine and liqueurs); *bruine krogen* (traditional "brown cafes"); or chic, style-conscious "designer" bars.

Bols Taverne. 106 Rozengracht. For Bols and many other characteristic Dutch drinks; also serves meals.

Cafe Américain. 28 Leidseplein; 624–5322. Popular and monumental Art Deco meeting place in the Hotel American.

Cafe Gollem. 4 Raamsteeg; 626–6645. The perfect place for beer lovers; has over 100 different beers, and calls itself a *bierakademie!*

Continental Bodega. 246 Lijnbaansgracht; 623–9098. Especially popular with the predinner drinks crowd, this old tasting house serves a wide array of dishes, but specializes in sherry from barrels numbered 1 to 10. Sippers on the mezzanine receive their orders via pulley from the bar below while enjoying live piano music. The top floor serves dinners until midnight.

Cox. Marnixstraat. A sunken designer bar in the artistic Stadsschouwburg building.

De Drie Fleschjes. 18 Gravenstraat; 624–8443. Another tasting house and one of the oldest, having opened in 1650. After a comprehensive tasting the visitor is not, perhaps, too unhappy that it closes at 8.30 P.M.

Land van Walem. 449 Keizersgracht. A place to be seen and to enjoy French-Dutch food.

Schiller. 242 N.Z. Voorburgwal. Comfortable and discreet tavern, the haunt of local intellectuals.

Brown Cafes

So named after the tobacco-smoke stained ceilings and walls that never seem to be redecorated, these are a must-see-and-sample aspect of Amsterdam. Great charm and character, in the best "pub" tradition. Among the best of these colorful Amsterdam institutions are:

Hoppe. 18–20 Spui. Crowded, rather louche bar.

De Koningshut. 269 Spui. Jovial atmosphere.

Het Laatste Oordeel. 17 Raadhuisstraat. Serves over 200 different beers!

Het Molenpad. 653 Prinsengracht. Friendly atmosphere and home cooking.

Papieeiland. 2 Prinsengracht. A typical tiled room in the Jordaan.

Reijnders. 6 Leidseplein. A mixed crowd from punks to professionals.

Scheltema. 242 N.Z. Voorburgwal. Comfortable old tavern.

NIGHTLIFE. Nightclubs in the traditional sense are practically nonexistent. Locals prefer pubs, clubs, dinner theater, discos, and gambling. What has become big business, mostly for tourists, are the topless bars (primarily around Rembrandtsplein) and the sex clubs in the red light district. The latter have been called more exciting that those in Hamburg. To the tourist they present a strange anomaly, because while on the one hand the Dutch have always been noted for a strict morality verging on puritanism, they are also stern upholders of absolute freedom. The wide wave of sexual freedom has certainly engulfed Amsterdam, where its effects are seen not only in the most bawdy nightclubs presenting every type of live show, but also in a rash of porno shops.

For obvious reasons, most of the way-out places do not advertise their location, and sources of information are the usual world-wide ones: hotel porter, taxi driver, head barman or waiter, who will certainly require a tip of, say Fl. 10. But beware—you may find yourself in a "live" show that just might shock you beyond your wildest expectations! Amsterdam also has a number of regular gay meeting places, many of them in and near the Kerkstraat, in which the heterosexual has been increasingly accepted during recent years. In Holland, homosexuality is anything but frowned on.

Nightlife is brightest around the Leidseplein and Rembrandtsplein, where the floorshows and discos only fill up after midnight. *Club La Mer,* 73 Korte Leidsedwarsstraat (tel. 624–2910) draws a trendy, young crowd into a stuffy cellar to dance to Motown and soul. *Zorba The Buddha,* 216 O.Z. Voorburgwal (tel. 675–9642), is run by the religious Baghwan sect in the heart of the red-light district; despite or because of this, the young only seem interested in dancing. *Mazzo,* 114 Rozengracht (tel. 626–7500) uses dramatic lighting and slick videos to attract poseurs and media types. *Juliana's,* 138 Apollolaan (tel. 673–7313), is an exclusive nightclub in the Hilton Hotel and the *Boston Club,* 1 Kattengat in the Sonesta Hotel (tel. 624–5561) caters to a sophisticated, older crowd.

All the nightclubs and bars within the three areas mentioned above can be regarded as safe for the tourist in a physical sense, though some may make heavy demands on your purse. The same goes for places recommended by your hotel porter. Wandering off on your own down side streets and back alleys is another matter, and one should be wary about touring the more insalubrious areas at night, especially those where the drug scene is active. This applies particularly to the area around the Central Station.

The regular nightclubs listed below are generally acceptable to all but the primmest of maiden aunts (although some go in for fairly spectacular striptease), and are as daring as the average person would want. Most are open from about 10 P.M. to 2 A.M. or even 4 A.M. and serve drinks which are not usually excessive in price. However, they might have moved or changed name, so check your choice with your hotel porter or even with the VVV. The alphabetical list below is not in order of merit or price.

De Amstel Taverne, 54 Amstel, close to Rembrandtsplein. A lively, long-established gay bar with music.

Bamboo Bar, 64 Lange Leidsedwarsstraat; 624–3993. Informal, inexpensive, relaxing and international. It boasts good jazz and blues around the longest bar in Amsterdam.

Le Berry Disco, 8 Leidseplein; 623–2156. Lots of action for the younger crowd (18–30).

BIMhuis, 73–77 Oude Schans; 623–3373. Set in a converted warehouse, this is currently the most fashionable jazz club. Sit in the adjoining BIM-cafe and enjoy a magical view across Oude Schans to the port. Open Thurs.–Sat.

Cab Kaye's Jazz Piano Bar, 9 Beulingstraat; 623–3594. A discreet place for jazz and singing. Open Tues.–Sat. until 3 A.M.

Carousel, 20 Thorbeckeplein. Informal, attended by the top people. Floorshow. Topless waitresses. Take your own instrument along if you have it, for you will be welcomed as a player.

Cul de Sac, 99 O.Z. Voorburgwal; 625–4548. A trendy bar in a 17th-century spice warehouse.

Disco Escape, 15 Rembrandtsplein; 622–3542. A huge dance floor and a lively pop scene; programs are recorded here for satellite T.V.

Joseph Lam Jazzclub, 8 Van Diemenstraat; 622–8086. Good Dixieland music. Near the old port, so go there by taxi. Open only on weekends.

Odeon, 460 Singel; 624–9711. A late-night, all-ages, drinking-and-dancing venue in a three-story former auction hall.

La Strada, 93 N.Z. Voorburgwal. 625–0276. A stylish women-only bar. Open until 3 A.M.

AMSTERDAM AS AN
EXCURSION CENTER

Holland in a Nutshell

There are few parts of the Netherlands that offer the variety of landscape and human activity that is characteristic of the region north and south of Amsterdam. Within the span of a single day you can roll the centuries back from Dudok's modern City Hall at Hilversum to a 13th-century castle at Muiden, from the modern North Sea beach resort of Zandvoort to the dreamy lassitude of Hoorn on the IJsselmeer. You can feast the eye with field after field of flowers, soothe the spirit with solitary walks through the west coast dunes, pursue the ghost of Frans Hals through the streets of Haarlem, and marvel at the wonder of a dike that stretches across open water for 32 km. (20 miles).

The province of Noord Holland that we plan to explore extends from the vast dike that encloses the IJsselmeer all the way south to a line that runs very roughly from the North Sea resort of Zandvoort east to Hilversum and then back up to the IJsselmeer again, thus encircling Amsterdam, the principal city and the capital of the country. For the sake of convenience, the island of Texel has been added to the northern limit of this territory and so have the bulbfields to the south, in the companion province of Zuid Holland.

Centuries ago there was no break between this peninsula and the mass of Friesland province on the far side of the IJsselmeer, which was then, as now, a lake. The city of Hoorn, for example, was once the capital of West Friesland though only 40 km. (25 miles) separate it from Amsterdam today. Little by little, however, the sea opened larger and larger breaches in the dunes that once continued north as far as the coast of Denmark. Erosion being a progressive process, the destruction of land proceeded at an even faster pace until West Friesland lay separated from the rest of Friesland by a water gap that was 16 km. (10 miles) wide at its narrowest. Had human ingenuity been unable to arrest this trend, the map of Noord Holland would look quite different today.

With modern skills and technology, however, the sea has been driven back. The first step was the completion of an enclosing dike in 1932 that turned the Zuiderzee into a lake, which has been rechristened the IJssel-meer. With the sea held at bay to the northwest, work has progressed on empoldering—diking off and pumping dry—the pear-shaped body of fresh water that was left to the south and east. The Noordoostpolder was com-pleted in 1942. The Oostelijk Flevoland Polder came dry in the spring of 1957 and the Zuidelijk (Southern) Flevoland Polder was pumped dry by 1968. Progress has been made on the Markerwaard Polder which would turn the present harbors of Volendam, Marken, Edam and Hoorn into small lakes and completely change their economy. The fear of this change is so great, however, that there is a strong degree of resistance among local people to the final draining of this polder, so the remaining area may still be left as a lake.

Exploring the Amsterdam Region

The first one-day tour takes us north up the east side of North Holland along the edge of the IJsselmeer to Volendam, Marken, Edam, Hoorn, Enkhuizen, Medemblik, and on as far as the enclosing dike. The second also runs north, but up the west or ocean coast through Zaandam and Alkmaar to Den Helder and the island of Texel. The third changes direc-tion and heads south to Aalsmeer, then west to the bulbfields, and finally back via Haarlem. The fourth turns east towards Muiden, Naarden, Hil-versum, Breukelen, and the Loosdrecht Lakes (dipping here briefly into the province of Utrecht). Readers who plan to drive around the IJsselmeer can include the first and fourth itineraries as part of that trip. We have also covered this interesting region with driving itineraries from two days to four days.

1—AMSTERDAM NORTH TO VOLENDAM, HOORN, AND THE ENCLOSING DIKE

Formerly the first stage of our 216-km. (134-mile) trip was by water, taking the ferry from Amsterdam across the IJ River to the road leading north. Today, however, we may drive over the Schellingwoude Bridge that spans the river to the northeast of the city or use the underwater IJ tunnel, preferably the latter except during rush hours. It is amazing how suddenly one is out of Amsterdam and into unspoilt country along this road.

Broek in Waterland is a scant 11 km. (7 miles) up the road. It seems more like a child's playground than a serious-minded community, perhaps because everything seems to be on a miniature scale. Still, it's one of the many towns where so-called Edam cheeses are produced, and if you are passing through in the summertime, you can watch them being made in the farmhouse of Jakob Wiedermeier & Son, just opposite the 15th-century church.

Hardly is the salty odor of curing cheeses out of the air than the towers of Monnickendam's Grote Kerk (Great Church) and Speeltoren signal our next stop. If it's a few minutes before the hour, hasten to Speeltoren, at Noordeinde 4, which is the tower of the 18th-century town hall. Instead of bells, a carillon chimes while two knights perform a solemn march. Unless they're stuck again. This building also houses the Archeological Museum. Take another moment to stroll down an avenue of dainty gabled houses to the harbor, and then, on your way back, note the finely detailed 17th-century Waag or Weigh House which is now a restaurant, offering smoked eels as a specialty.

Out of Monnickendam to the east is a small road leading to the fishing village of Marken; once an island, it is now connected to the mainland by a 3 km. (2 mile) long causeway. In spite of its obvious dedication to being a tourist attraction, it is a delightful village, its streets small traffic-free paths and an occasional person still in traditional costume. Despite the comment of one so-called expert that "the baggy knee breeches of the Markenaars give them the look of boatmen from Greece," the effect is more Oriental than Mediterranean. The women's flowered chintzes, inspired by the East Indies, are one reason for the impression. The children were traditionally dressed alike in skirts up to the age of six, the boys being identifiable by the color of their skirts—blue. Unfortunately for visitors, the youngsters are nowadays seldom seen in traditional dress. But on April 30th everyone is dressed in orange costumes to celebrate Queen's Day. Marken had no choice but to become a tourist village: when the Zuiderzee was enclosed in 1932, the island's fishing income disappeared and tourism was the only option.

Besides costumes, one of the chief attractions here are the houses that line Marken's narrow streets. Seafaring traditions have obviously influenced their construction, with the result that the interiors are as compact and tidy as the cabin of a ship. This nautical overtone has been muted, however, by the porcelain, clocks, glassware, hangings, and other furnishings that have been passed down the ages. Have a look at the Marken Museum for a recreation of the fishermen's cottages typical until 1932. Notice the whitewashed walls, the room with a hole in the roof to let the smoke escape.

Similarly, look inside the church, where model ships in full sail hang from the ceiling. Remember that Marken, a strict Reformed community, observes the Sabbath to the letter.

From Marken, return to Monnickendam by road and continue north 6 km. (3½ miles) to Volendam, the hub of tourism in this much-frequented region. Instead of getting to Marken along the causeway mentioned above, it is possible to leave your car at Volendam and take a motorlaunch. The trip along the waterfront, lined with old Dutch houses and shops, takes about 25 minutes each way.

A Roman Catholic village in contrast to the Protestant fishermen on the island of Marken, Volendam makes a business out of wearing traditional costumes and encouraging tourists to take pictures. The men sport baggy pantaloons that are fastened with silver guilders instead of buttons. Over these are worn red-and-white-striped jackets and a cap. The women, in turn, have the appearance of birds in flight, thanks to the pointed wings on their white lace bonnets. It is rumored that some of these caps are now made of drip-dry, no-iron nylon, but no one will admit such sacrilege, yet. Be on the lookout for the *zevenkleurige rok* or seven-colored skirt. On Sundays a different costume is worn that is more elaborate. There are frequent boat trips to Marken.

We continue north 5 km. (3 miles) more along the top of the sea dike to Edam, a picturesque and tranquil little town with a population of 22,000. The center is crossed by canals that have drawbridges and are lined with old houses that boast lovely façades. Edam was once an important port, but today it is best known for its cheese, which is famous all over the world for its distinctive ball-like shape and red skin. These are the characteristics of the exported variety; in Holland Edam cheese is sold with a yellow skin. It is, in fact, produced in a number of provinces. First stop, perhaps, in Edam should be the fascinating Captain's House on the Dam just opposite the Town Hall, now the Edam Museum. Paintings that hang on the walls of its front room will introduce you to some of the town's more remarkable citizens. Most imposing is the lifesize, full-length portrait of Trijntje Kester who was nearly 4 meters (13 feet) tall at the age of seventeen. Pieter Dirksz is equally arresting, thanks to a forked red beard so long that he had to fold it over his arm. Although this triumph was possibly a handicap under some circumstances, it didn't prevent his election as mayor.

As you clamber up and down the narrow stairs, peer into the bunk-like beds built into the walls, and stand on the "bridge" with its view of the rooms below, you will see many items of daily usage back in the 18th century. During summer, the *Kaaswaag* or Weigh House features a display on the making of local cheeses.

The 18th-century Town Hall that faces this remarkable building has a green and gold council chamber that ranks it among the most beautiful of all Holland's civic rooms and an impressive wedding hall.

The original Grote Kerk, or Great Church, dating from the 15th century, was almost completely destroyed by fire and had to be rebuilt in 1602 and again in 1670. It has a stately charm and some unusually fine stained-glass windows, and has now been fully restored and reopened to the public each afternoon.

Another great attraction is the bell tower that carries a lovely carillon. This tower was once part of a Catholic church that was destroyed. The tower was left standing, but only just, for a few years ago it began to lean dangerously. The area was evacuated and the tower made safe. It still leans a bit, but not so much as its counterpart in Pisa. The carillon was cast in Mechelen in 1561, and is one of the oldest in the country. From Edam boat trips are available to nearby Purmerend, site of the Thursday cheese market in summer (11 A.M.–1 P.M.), and out across the IJsselmeer.

Hoorn, Ancient Shipping Center

Leaving Edam by road, you continue through rural landscapes along the 18 km. (11 miles) that separate it from Hoorn. You can also continue to follow the sea dike from Edam to Hoorn, but its twistings and turnings require three times as long to navigate.

Don't rush through Hoorn, however. It is certainly not a "dead city"—at least there's nothing ghostlike about the 56,000 people who live there today—and who can tell what its future will be if the Markerwaard Polder places it in the midst of rich farm country? Its development was abruptly arrested in the 17th century when England, not limited to flat-bottomed boats that could clear the sandbanks of the IJsselmeer, eclipsed Holland in the shipping trade. Its importance as a port further declined with the completion of the Noordhollandskanaal linking Amsterdam directly to the sea. Today it is a rapidly growing commuter community and yacht harbor that takes pride in its maritime legacy.

Willem Cornelis Schouten (1580–1625) was born here. In 1616 he was the first to round the southern tip of South America, which he named Cape Hoorn (later Horn) in honor of his home town. Another native, Jan Pieterszoon Coen (1587–1629) founded Batavia (now Jakarta), in Java, governed the island from 1617 to his death, and did much to establish Holland's empire in the East Indies. Later, Abel Janszoon Tasman (1603–59) circumnavigated Australia, discovered New Zealand, and gave his name to the island of Tasmania. Here, too, on October 11, 1573, the combined fleets of Hoorn, Enkhuizen, Edam, and Monnikendam defeated a Spanish force within sight of the ramparts and brought the Spanish Admiral Bossu back a prisoner.

To explore Hoorn in a leisurely manner, park your car by the train station and walk along the Kleine Noord, the 15th-century Noorderkerk (North Church) St. Mary's is on your left. A carved panel inside dated 1642 has a horn on each side, the one separating the words *wilt* and *'t-woort,* the other *gaat* and *'t-woort.* Since Hoorn is pronounced the same as *horen* (the verb "hear"), the inscription is a pun: "Be willing to hear the Word," and "Go hear the Word." Inside the church is a miniature model of the town. Stop here and see the Sound and Light Show that takes you back to Hoorn in 1650 (June–mid-Sept.).

In a moment you enter the Rode Steen or Kaasmarkt, the chief square, with a statue of the aforementioned Coen in the middle, the 1609 Waag or Weigh House on the left. This is another of Hendrick de Keyser's buildings; today it houses a restaurant. The 1632 Westfries Museum is on the right in an impressive building, a museum since 1932, on the Rode Steen Square. Its gable is decorated with the coats-of-arms of the seven cities of West Friesland whose delegates once met here.

A lovely fireplace is to be found in the Grote Voorzaal, the hall, as well as several fine guild paintings. A collection of antiques and artifacts of great beauty are exhibited on the first floor, brought here during the 17th century by the East India Company, and there is also a portrait of Admiral de Ruyter by Bol (1667). In addition, there are weapons, armor, silver, porcelain, flags, coins, and much else associated with the history of Hoorn and its region. The whole of the second floor is dedicated to the maritime past of the town.

Turn left down the Grote Oost street, lined by houses whose façades incline perilously forward, perhaps to keep the rain off passers-by, perhaps to flatter the vanity of owners who wanted the ornate fronts to be more easily seen. At the end on the right, just before you cross the canal, are three houses with a frieze that re-creates the sea battle in which Bossu was defeated. Continue across the bridge through Kleine Oost to the East Gate, completed in 1578, the house on top dating from 1601. An inscription in Latin reads: "Neither the watchfulness of the guards, nor the arms, nor the threatening walls, nor the thunder of the hoarse cannon will avail anything, if thou, God, wilt not rule and shelter this town."

Retrace your steps down the Kleine Oost, cross the bridge again, and this time turn left along Slapershaven. Directly ahead is another bridge and, beyond, a house with an unusual façade and 1624 over the door. Next door is the meeting place of the West India Company in 1784.

Follow Oude Doelenkade around the curve of the inner harbor, and you'll see the remarkable tower of the Hoofdtoren, part of the harbor defences of the town and dating from 1532. The belfry on top was added 119 years later. During the 17th century it housed the offices of a company that financed whaling expeditions to the Arctic, a theme commemorated in a carved oak chimney-piece that is now in the Westfries Museum. Note here the row of beautifully restored 17th-century houses along the Veermanskade.

Returning to the central square, we head down Nieuwstraat a short block to Kerkplein. On the left at No. 39 is the Sint Jansgasthuis or St. John's Hospital, a beautiful early Renaissance building with the date 1563, which housed the ill and infirm for more than three hundred years. A plaque on the wall commemorates five Dutch people who were killed by the Germans in 1945. At the next left-hand corner of Nieuwstraat and Nieuwsteeg is the Town Hall with not one but two stepped gables. A Hieronymite convent was established here in 1385, traces of which can be identified in the present 1613 structure. The magnificent Council Room inside is enlivened with a painting representing the naval victory over Bossu.

From here we turn half-left down Gouw, then left again on Gedempte Turfhaven (Filled-in Peat-harbor), until we see a block away on the right, the entrance to Sint Pietershof with the date 1691. Go inside for an impression of one of the most charming of Holland's many almshouses or old people's homes. A convent predating 1461 once stood here, then an old men's home. In 1639 it was incorporated into an old women's home, and is still in use.

A craft market is held in Hoorn every Wednesday from late June until mid-August. Stalls are arranged around the market place with a glassblower, glass painter, lacemaker, weaver, brass worker, sculptor and many others demonstrating their traditional skills. Folk dancing adds a festive flavor to the market. Hoorn also has one of the busiest pleasure boating harbors in Holland, attracting over 20,000 visiting yachts a year. Yachts can be rented and sailing trips organized.

The journey between Hoorn and Medemblik can be made by antique steam train, which operates during the summer. One can also hire "Zuiderseebotter", traditional fishermen's sailing craft, for an outing on the water. Antiques are a popular buy in Hoorn, from organs to tiles or old ship equipment.

Enkhuizen and the Zuiderzee Museum

Another 19 km. (12 miles) bring us to a second IJsselmeer port that has declined from roughly 50,000 souls in the 17th century to about 16,000 today. Enkhuizen's herring fleet once numbered 400 vessels, setting sail not far from the massive double tower called De Drommedaris or Dromedar (1540) whose carillon ranks next to that of Edam. The silting up of the Zuiderzee at the end of the 17th century made Enkhuizen a romantic but dead place until this century. Of interest are the 1688 Town Hall, with a museum on the second floor, and the Stedelijk Waagmuseum, built in 1559, situated at the Kaasmarkt (cheese market). It is the old Weigh House in which cheese and butter auctions took place. Today it is a small municipal museum. We then continue to the waterside and the Binnen-museum Zuiderzeemuseum, appropriately lodged in the Peperhuis, a former warehouse of the East India Company. Here have been gathered together exhibits that explain much about the fishing, furniture, costumes, architecture, and topography of the entire region that today bears the name of the IJsselmeer. When you have admired the heavy timbers and solid workmanship of the three-centuries-old building, studied the sample rooms with their authentically dressed dummies, marveled over the manner of men who used cannon-size shotguns to decimate a flight of geese, step out the back door and examine the boats and yachts of all periods that are tied up at the pier to illustrate the history of shipbuilding. A large covered hall of ships is being added to with new finds, proving that for centuries, even from Roman times, the IJsselmeer has been the graveyard of ships of all sizes and types. Holland's great problem now is to find space in which to display what are undoubtedly remarkable historical and archeological discoveries. The Wapenmuseum, or Museum of Weapons, has been established in the old prison, which has a picturesque façade dating from 1612.

The greatest touristic achievement in Enkhuizen is the open-air Buiten-museum Zuiderzeemuseum. Some 130 original 17th-century buildings, farmhouses, shops, public offices and even a church have been collected from villages and towns around the old Zuiderzee and reerected along the cobbled streets of this museum, which was first opened in 1983 by the Queen. You reach the Buitenmuseum by ferry from the Enkhuizen-Lelystad dike car park.

On the west edge of town the main road leads left. We keep straight ahead, however, following the signs for Bovenkarspel and Grootebroek. At Hoogkarspel we turn right and follow the country roads north for a total of 21 km. (13 miles) to Medemblik, the third and smallest of our dreaming IJsselmeer cities. We now pass the restored Radboud Castle (Kasteel), which was built in the 8th century by the Frisian King Radboud. In 1288 Count Floris V fortified the castle to keep his recently-conquered Frisian subjects from rebelling. The interior of the castle has been restored to its original state and it is open daily from May 15 to September 15, 10–5, and on Sundays only, 2–5, for the remainder of the year. The Eerste Nederlandse Stoommachinemuseum is devoted to a fine collection of early steam engines and housed, appropriately enough, in a former steam-powered pumping station.

Also of note in Medemblik is the fine Gothic Bonifaciuskerk, with some late-17th-century stained glass windows and an early-Gothic gate.

As you leave town by the Medemblikkerweg leading northwest to the main highway, keep your eye cocked for the Lely pumping station on the right at some distance from the road. We are now entering the Wieringermeer Polder, completed in 1930, and it was one of the two stations used to pump the water out. It has the unbelievable capacity of 1,500,000 litres (330,000 gallons) per *minute*, yet when you consider that much of the

20,235 hectares (50,000 acres) reclaimed here are 6 meters (18 feet) below sea level, the need for such a vast potential becomes evident.

Three towns were built in the midst of this pentagon-shaped polder: Slootdorp, Middenmeer, and Wieringerwerf. The highway leads us past the last of these, about 6 km. (4 miles) west of the point where the Germans breached the dike on April 17, 1945, only 18 days before the Nazi surrender. The land, of course, was completely flooded, but the polder was pumped dry as soon as the dike had been repaired, and crops were growing again in the fields by the following spring and half the houses were saved.

Twenty-three kilometers (14 miles) after leaving Medemblik we pass a second pumping station at the northern end of Wieringermeer Polder and cross a corner of the former island of Wieringen to the town of Den Oever, the beginning of the Afsluitdijk or enclosing dike.

Although many men dreamed of running a barrier from Noord Holland to Friesland and reclaiming the IJsselmeer, Dr. Lely was the first to conceive a practical plan, back in 1891. Persuading the government to appropriate the funds required an additional 25 years. Actual work commenced in 1923. The dike you see today is 29 km. (18 miles) long, 92 meters (300 feet) wide, and 6 meters (21 feet) above mean water level. Its top carries a surfaced motor road plus a path for bicycles and another for pedestrians.

At a point slightly more than halfway across, a monument raises its tower above the point at which the dike was closed on May 28, 1932. From its top you can survey the entire project from shore to shore on a fine day, and, if the daring of the scheme has caught your imagination, buy an illustrated booklet describing this and a number of other reclamation plans. Then, turning back after a pause at the café in the base of the monument, we start the 89-km. (55-mile) run back to Amsterdam.

But the Dutch have found more than romance and history in their old IJsselmeer. Apart from the large areas of new land being reclaimed from that historic basin of water, they are now using it for hydraulic studies as well. On the eastern side, near Emmen, the Delft Hydraulics Laboratory has established a large open-air and covered experimental station in which extensive model studies are carried out not only for current and planned Dutch projects but also for hydraulic works intended for countries all over the world.

II—AMSTERDAM NORTHWEST TO ZAANDAM, ALKMAAR, AND TEXEL

This excursion is shorter than the first—183 km. (114 miles)—and takes us up the west coast of Noord Holland to Den Helder, terminus for the boats to Texel (which there won't be time to visit in a single day), then back down through the center of the province to Amsterdam. We are completely away from the IJsselmeer with its memories of days of glory.

We leave Amsterdam by the road that leads to Zaanstad, via the Coentunnel underneath the Noordzee Kanaal or North Sea Canal, another of the mighty engineering works of the Dutch. You'll recall that originally Amsterdam's ships reached the open sea by sailing east to the IJsselmeer and then north. The silting of the IJsselmeer during the 18th century, however, threatened Amsterdam (where during the Golden Age more than 3,000 ships could be counted alongside the busy quays) with extinction unless some new outlet were discovered that could accommodate vessels of deep draft. The North Sea Canal was the solution.

Extending for 24 km. (15 miles) through dunes whose average height is 10 meters (33 feet) above sea level, it reaches the ocean at the fishing village of IJmuiden after passing through a set of locks so vast that the *QE 2* could pass through with 45 meters (150 feet) to spare at each end. The canal itself was opened in 1876 after 11 years of labor; the present system of locks was completed in 1930 and can cope with a difference in water level of 4 meters (13 feet), although the average is normally about half that. So much salt water is admitted every time the locks are used that the entire IJsselmeer could be contaminated if there were not another set of locks at the Amsterdam end to keep the waterway isolated. The entrance was recently enlarged to accommodate tankers.

For many years the canal had the effect of cutting Noord Holland in half and leaving road traffic dependent on ferries. In 1957, however, a vehicular tunnel was completed in Velsen, and later the Coentunnel and the IJ tunnel were finished, giving Amsterdam better connections with northern parts.

The Zaan area, which we enter after crossing the canal, was Holland's great windmill area centuries ago, and although hundreds have been torn down, after being replaced by modern pump engines, you will still see a few scattered here and there. Even more important, if you play golf, is the fact that the district gave birth to the game of *kolf,* considered by many to be the lineal ancestor of today's pastime. There is little resemblance to today's game; then only one club was used which looked like a rather unfortunate combination of hockey stick and polo mallet. The ball, a clumsy leather affair, was half again bigger than a cricket ball or soft ball. You can see some of these primitive implements, by the way, at Den Haag Golf and Country Club.

During the 17th century Holland was renowned as the leading ship-building nation of the world, with Zaandam as its center. One of the many people who came here to study Dutch progress in ship-building, mathematics and physics at first hand was Peter the Great, the enlightened young Czar of All the Russias. Arriving "incognito" in Zaandam in 1697, he worked in the shipyards as Peter Michailov, but local curiosity forced him to take refuge in Amsterdam after one week. Czar Nicholas II (1868–1918) arranged to have the small wooden house his ancestor had inhabited during his short stay in Zaandam turned into a museum, now called Het Czaar Peterhuisje, and in 1911 he presented the town with a statue of Czar Peter, which now adorns the marketplace.

A few kilometers up the road is Koog aan de Zaan, notable chiefly for the old (1751) Het Pink windmill, an oil mill that is operated by volunteers from time to time, usually on the fourth Saturday of the month. At Zaandijk, a village just east of the highway, is an antiquities museum, called Zaanlandse Oudheidkamer, housed in the 18th-century home of a wealthy merchant. Its rooms are furnished in the typical old *Zaanse* style and represent the life, culture and industry of the district in former times. Even more interesting is De Zaanse Schans, the windmill village. Strolling round the green Zaan houses and the windmills you'll find yourself back in the 17th century. Definitely worth visiting are an historic grocery shop, a former merchant's home containing period rooms, a bakery museum, clock museum, and wooden clog workshop. On three Saturdays in May, it is possible to go by boat to visit the De Reef bird sanctuary (tel. 075–16221).

This Zaan area, however, has not escaped the Dutch industrial revolution. Side by side with the old buildings still redolent of clever craftsmanship there are now busy factories turning out a host of different products. Yet every effort is being made to retain some of the old-time glamor of the area.

We continue along a secondary road (not the expressway) to Krommenie, a hamlet where everything seems to be on a miniature scale. Gables, pilasters, façades, cornucopias, and sculptured panels abound in this arcadia of two-roomed cottages. Particularly interesting are the houses at 74 Noorder Hoofdstraat and at 65 and 115 Zuider Hoofdstraat.

If it's spring, take the old Alkmaar highway (N203) and stop at Limmen, a center of the tulip, narcissus, and hyacinth industry. Here, at 64 Dusseldorperweg, is *Hortus Bulborum,* a unique outdoor "tulip museum" in which practically all the original varieties of this wonderful flower are still preserved—and grown. If not, turn north at Uitgeest and follow the country road to Akersloot, the oldest village in this part of the Netherlands according to records that date back to 777. Even more impressive, however, is the Alkmaarder Lake on which it lies, a yachting center crowded with graceful craft. Beyond Akersloot the road follows the west side of a canal all the way into Alkmaar.

Alkmaar and Its Cheese Market

Though Alkmaar is famous today for the Friday-morning cheese market (mid-April to mid-September), it is worth visiting in its own right, too. Its origins go back to the 9th century, but its proudest day was October 8th, 1573 when Don Frederico of Toledo, son of the dreaded Duke of Alva, was forced to abandon his siege of the town. This was the first important victory over the Spanish, the first indication that the Dutch could hope to succeed in throwing off the foreign yoke. The event is still celebrated on this date, with carnivals and street festivities.

The late 15th-century St. Laurenskerk (St. Lawrence's Church) has one of the finest antique organs in the Netherlands, a plaque commemorating Count Floris V, who overcame the fierce Frisians and built the castle at Medemblik. The Town Hall, a beautiful Gothic building from 1520, contains the meeting room of the mayor and corporation, in Renaissance style and can be visited when it is not otherwise in use. Its original wood ceiling from 1634 is striking. The Stedelijk Museum is in a historic building, Nieuwe Doelen, built in the early 16th century for the National Guard, and housing a collection of old toys, maps and pictures. But the glory of Alkmaar is the Waaggebouw or Weigh House. Originally a chapel, its steep gables draw the eye upward by a labyrinth of receding planes that culminate in the weathervane.

If it's a Friday morning, it won't be easy to tear yourself from the spectacle taking place at your feet. The cheeses arrive at the market by truck (the factory may be as little as one kilometer away), and are unloaded by means of a juggling act that would do credit to any circus as the round balls, weighing 2–6.5 kg. (4–14 lb.), are transferred to barrows that look vaguely like stretchers. At this point the porters or carriers take over. Together they form an ancient guild with the exclusive privilege of handling the cheeses. A "father" directs the activities of the 28 porters and various older workers who assist them. The porters, in turn, are divided into four groups or *veems*. Each group consists of three pairs of carriers and a silver-badged headman who is responsible for seeing that his men are spotless, punctual, and well disciplined, and that the group's scales are correct.

The actual selling of the cheeses takes place in a ring and is consummated by a handclasp that is as binding on both parties as a signed contract. The porters wait until a barrow is piled high with cannonball-sized cheeses. They then attach a leather shoulder sling to the barrow's handles and jog off with a distinctive bobbing gait calculated not to spill the load. At the weighroom the barrow is set on the group's own scales. The total is noted on a blackboard, and then the barrow is carried off to the new owner of the cheeses.

All morning long the twelve pairs of porters jog their way through the crowds of tourists to the Waaggebouw, or Weigh House, and back, gradually building up their tally for the day. The color group with the highest total is made chief guild group until the following week. When the market is over, the porters retire to their own quarters to drink beer, using centuries-old pewter mugs that have been handed down from father to son. Over the fireplace hangs a "shame board" with the names of the men who were late reporting to work or who cursed while on duty. The Waaggebouw was once a Chapel of the Holy Ghost, built in the early 14th century, which served as a refuge for needy travelers. It was transformed into a Weigh House in 1582 after Alkmaar's weighing rights were restored.

During the Kaasmarkt, between 11 and 12 noon, the 35-bell carillon bursts into life with a medley of tunes that cascade down the belfry in a golden shower. As a finale, the noon hour is announced, and at every stroke of the bell, a trumpeter blows his horn, doors open, and horsemen burst out of the clock tower, lances held high. Other one-hour concerts are at 6.30 P.M. on Thursday and 1.30 P.M. on Sunday.

For 300 years cheese has been sold in this fashion at Alkmaar. If today the market is perpetuated for the benefit of tourists (more efficient ways of handling cheese have been developed over the centuries), it is done with a zest that betrays the townspeople's own delight in recalling bygone days when there was time for pageantry. Before leaving town, visit with the legendary Hans Brinker. A museum named for this fictional character includes displays of skates and local lore. You can also tour the waterways by open boat.

Close to Alkmaar lies the pleasant village of Bergen, on the edge of the sea dunes and beside a forest. A gently meandering path leads through the dunes to the sea. For the past century Dutch artists have settled here where life is pleasant and the surroundings inspiring. On the village square is an artists' center, with exhibition room and work for sale. Every Friday in July and August an art market is held here. Roughly 5 km. (3 miles) due west is Bergen aan Zee, a simple, family-type seaside resort similar to Egmond aan Zee and Castricum aan Zee, which lie farther down the coast to the south.

We follow a local road north, however, towards Schoorl, skirting the edge of the widest and most densely wooded dunes in the Netherlands. We pass through sleepy villages—Bregtdorp, Katrijp, Hargen, Camperduin—that curve gently westward until suddenly we are face to face with the North Sea. Ahead of us stretches a 5-km. (3-mile) gap in the dunes that has been heavily reinforced with piles, breakwaters, and dikes with the collective name of Hondsbosse Zeewering. The road runs alongside the fortifications to Petten, which has been twice submerged by the sea.

The coastal road ducks back behind a new range of dunes for another 10 km. (6 miles) to the dreamy seaside resort of Callantsoog. From there it's a straight run into Den Helder at the northernmost tip of Noord Holland between, in season, fields vivid with tulips and the arrow-straight canal.

Den Helder and Texel Island

Bordered by the rolling North Sea on three sides, set among extensive bulb fields that bloom during April and May, and secure behind heavy dikes, Den Helder is full of surprises. At the end of the 18th century it was a forgotten fishing village visited by seagulls. Then, in January 1794, the Dutch fleet got itself frozen into the ice between Den Helder and Texel Island opposite. A detachment of French cavalry took advantage of this predicament by riding out on the ice and capturing the fleet, one of the few instances in naval warfare when horsemen have been decisive. Five years later the Duke of York landed here with a force of 13,000 Russian and 10,000 English troops, who were subsequently defeated near Bergen by French and Dutch forces based on Alkmaar. In 1811, Napoleon ordered the town fortified.

Today Den Helder is the chief Dutch naval base and training center, recruiting many men and women from the sturdy citizens of the city itself. The Royal Naval College, the Admiralty Palace, an interesting Maritime Museum, the state shipyards, and usually a contingent of vessels can be seen. Standing on the quay you can recall that glorious day in 1673 when a Dutch fleet under the command of admirals Tromp and De Ruyter defeated a combined English and French fleet almost within sight of this coast.

Texel, the largest—25 km. (15 miles) long, 10 (6) wide—and most southerly of the five Wadden Islands, is a scant 3 km. (2 miles) from Den Helder. A good ferry service carrying passengers and cars makes the 20-minute run to the port of 't Horntje. You might prefer to leave your car in the free parking area in front of the ferry terminal in Den Helder and take the passenger ferry. On the other side there are frequent buses from the 't Horntje terminal to different parts of the island, and bikes can be rented for Fl. 7.50 daily or Fl. 20 a week. This is also a more economical way to see the island. Less than 13,000 people live in the seven villages scattered about its surface, although during the year it has millions and millions of visitors. For Texel is a bird paradise, a breeding ground (May and June) discovered by the birds themselves and now protected by the island authorities. Its wide dunes, extensive moors, shallow lakes, and wooded clumps form ideal seasonal homes for mating, breeding, and training the young as part of that great miracle of nature known as migration. In the spring the visitors arrive by the million. Almost every known variety of duck and geese, belligerent ruffs and peaceful reeves, avocets and plovers, wagtails and warblers, stately spoonbills and dignified herons, kestrels and bitterns, blue herons, oyster-catchers and the short-eared owl. These are just a few of the regulars who turn this island into a bird-lover's treasure-house. Sick birds (and seals) are treated at a special hospital in the Nature Recreation Center in De Koog. The guides who conduct the human visitors around these sanctuaries know just how far the different bird colonies will tolerate inquisitiveness. For the special benefit of bird-lovers the Texel VVV has prepared a brochure on the bird life of the island, including a survey of the different reserves and a checklist of those which can be seen. If you decide to stay here for a few days, there are a number of smallish hotels, some of which make special arrangements for bird watchers, including excursions.

But don't expect to rush around Texel. This is an isle of peace, where you are expected to move quietly, to take your time to see the flocks of sheep grazing so placidly on its pasture, or the millions of narcissi blooming in spring, or its fishing fleet, or farmers who make their special green cheese from ewe milk.

On Texel you can ride, cycle, walk, or take a bus. The seven villages are linked by good though narrow roads, and the rolling dunes and golden beaches are unhampered by restrictions on walking or bathing or picnicking, except in those areas left undisturbed for the birds' breeding grounds.

The whole transport system of the island covering the ferry and bus services are owned by Teso which stands for Texel's Eigen Stoomboot Onderneming, meaning Texel's Own Steamship Society. Owned by the local population, it began by opening the steamer service, and the profits from its activities mainly go towards improving the roads, educational facilities and health schemes of the island. Teso runs several large and modern drive-on-drive-off vessels, giving an hourly service: although in busy periods there is a trip every half hour. Reservation of space is neither necessary nor possible. The journey is a pleasant one and makes it possible to get from Amsterdam to Texel in about two hours.

Over recent years there has been a battle between those who would like to drill for oil and natural gas here, and conservationists. The conservationists have largely won, with the water between mainland and islands being declared a protected area. For recreation there is swimming, sailing and angling along the dikes for which a permit is needed, obtainable from the post office. It is also possible to camp among the dunes, as many do during summer. In August and September a popular sport is "mud-walking" (*wadlopen*), the Dutch answer to mountain climbing! At certain times of day the Wadden Sea becomes a dryish mudflat and is safe to cross with an experienced guide. Halfway across the seabed, the vertical shapes fall away and there is nothing but flatness in all directions. (Sneakers and shorts are recommended).

The Den Burg VVV office has prepared a *Birdwalk* leaflet describing a 35-mile walk; birdwatching excursions are organized by the State Forest Dept. Bookings can be made through the Nature Recreation Centre, 92 Ruyslaan, De Koog. Also get the VVV brochure entitled *Bird Sanctuaries*. Texel is also renowned for its folk festival which reaches its peak on April 30th, Queen's Day, and also a crowd pleaser, a Jazz Festival in June.

South to Broek op Langedijk

The quickest way back to Amsterdam from Den Helder is via the main highway Alkmaar and Zaanstad, which we have been following or skirting all day. Instead, let's take an extra hour or two to explore a series of country roads and the simple farming communities.

Ten kilometers (six miles) south of Den Helder a left-hand fork leads east to Anna Paulowna, a town strung along the waters of a canal that drains a polder of the same name, honoring the Russian Grand Duchess who married Willem, Prince of Orange, later King Willem II, in 1816. A sharp turn takes us south again until we join a better road at Schagen, which, along with Texel, is the scene of a weekly folklore pageant during July and August. Then southeast to Oude Niedorp and to Noordscharwoude, the beginning of a remarkable 5-km. (3-mile) community that changes its name to Zuidscharwoude and then Broek op Langedijk. On the other side of the main highway, between Bergen and Heerhugowaard, you will find one of the biggest artificial ski-slopes in Europe.

This is the region of a thousand islands. A maze of canals tied together by a web of lovely bridges greets the eye, together with Frisian gondolas gliding back and forth carrying farmers and vast loads. Chances are they are all bound in one direction, towards the auction hall that claims to be the world's oldest (1887), largest, and most remarkable vegetable market. This is now a living museum "Broeker Veiling," Broek op Langedijk, where you can buy your fruit, vegetables and flowers at auction.

Below Broek op Langedijk we rejoin a main highway for another 5 km. (3 miles). When it forks right for Alkmaar, we turn left and follow an arrowlike country road east across the middle of the Schermer Polder, whose midpoint is marked by the village of Stompetoren. Just before entering Schermerhorn, we climb out of this polder only to descend, just beyond, into the even older (1612) Beemster Polder, perhaps the most beautiful in all Holland. This is an orchard area whose fruit trees burst into blossom between the end of April and early May. Some of the original farmhouses still stand, bearing such dates as 1682 and 1695, and can be seen on the right-hand side of the road less than two kilometers south of Midden Beemster.

Working our way east around the right-angle corners of this gridiron-shaped paradise, we soon enter Purmerend, which stands on high ground in the middle of the Beemster, Purmer, and Wormer polders. The church, which dates back to 1358, has been extensively restored and has a fine baroque organ (1742), but the major attractions are the tremendous pig, cattle, and horse market on Tuesday mornings and the historical Kaasmarkt. The cheese market is centuries old and is held at the foot of the Town Hall. Every Thursday morning, 11–1 P.M., during July and August, cheese porters, dressed usually in white with only blue or red ribbon distinguishing their guild, and sporting straw hats, show the public how they taste, weigh and buy the cheese.

From Purmerend a 16-km. (10-mile) stretch of highway leads back to Amsterdam.

III—AMSTERDAM SOUTH TO AALSMEER, THE BULBFIELDS, AND HAARLEM

This is the shortest of our excursions—112 km. (70 miles) if the bulbfields are in bloom, otherwise 77 (48)—and the most beautiful. Hardly are we out of Amsterdam on the main highway leading south to Den Haag and Rotterdam than we drop down into the Haarlemmermeer Polder, the largest and most important in the Netherlands until the enclosing dike was completed. For centuries the former Haarlemmermeer Lake—23 km. (14 miles) long—was a constant threat to Haarlem and even Amsterdam as well as to the ships that sailed across or fished in its waters. A gale or even a sudden change of wind was enough to pile its waves against the dikes along its sides.

As early as 1617, one of Holland's most talented engineers and windmill designers, Jan Adriaansz Leeghwater, conceived a plan for diking and draining the Haarlemmermeer. The book in which he described his scheme for using 160 windmills went through seventeen editions, but the capital investment required was too great for those days and the success of so ambitious an undertaking was too problematic. Not until 1851 with the advent of steam powered pumps did his dream become a reality.

We head out of Amsterdam on the main highway (A4) between the Dutch capital and The Hague. The road dives into a tunnel beneath one of the runways of Schiphol Airport, which lies located in the northeast corner of this vast polder, a circumstance that makes it unlike any other airfield in the world. Its runways are 4 meters (13 feet) below sea level.

Schiphol is the most important commercial airport in the country and one of the busiest and best-equipped airports in Europe. Currently, it is in the throes of a multibillion guilder expansion in preparation for the 21st century. The surrounding farmlands are quickly being transformed into a high-tech distribution center to handle the surge in air cargo, an important industry for this country. At Schiphol is the national aviation museum Aviodome, with its striking aluminum dome. It contains displays depicting man's adventures in the air since the days of the Wright brothers, with many early planes as well as scale models of aircraft and space ships, along with information on the future plans for the surrounding region.

Past the entrance to Schiphol, we continue to the exit for Aalsmeer, then right to 313 Legmeerdijk in Aalsmeer, the site of the world's largest auction hall (Verenigde Bloemenveilingen Aalsmeer). The building, which is equivalent in size to 77 U.S. football fields, contains six auction rooms where more than 50,000 transactions a day take place, one every two or three seconds. Buyers begin bidding as early as 7.30 A.M. and continue until everything has been sold, usually about 11.30 A.M. five days a week. In a single year up to three billion flowers and 220 million plants are sold here, coming from over 4,000 nurseries. This district is also one of the largest flower growing centers in the world, with 270 hectares (667 acres) of greenhouses. Annual turnover is around Fl. 1.8 billion. From the visitors' gallery, in the auction hall, you can watch this fascinating spectacle.

The flowers arrive by truck and are sorted out into lots. A sample is selected from each lot and held up for the assembled buyers to see. The auctioneer then sets in motion what looks like a vast clock with numbers around the rim and in the middle. The numbers in the middle correspond to the seats in which the buyers sit, each of which has an electric button. The numbers around the rim represent prices for ten bunches of flowers or plants similar to the sample being displayed. A pointer, like a huge minute-hand, begins to move, but instead of starting at low prices and working up, it begins at high prices and moves backwards—a Dutch auction. The instant it reaches a price acceptable to the most eager buyer, he presses his button, the minute-hand stops, and the number of his seat lights up on the clock face. This proceeds at the rate of roughly 600 lots per hour.

Once sold, the flowers are taken to the packing and delivery sheds. Those intended for export are skilfully wrapped in tissue and lightweight cardboard boxes, rushed to nearby Schiphol Airport, and are being admired in Stockholm, Paris, and London flowershop windows before the end of the day, all within 12 hours of the time they were cut. Those for sale in Holland and other nearby countries are loaded in trucks and dispatched to shops all over northern Europe.

Even in the depths of winter when the roads are slick with ice and the canals half frozen, bargefuls of huge cherry chrysanthemums, roses, carnations, and lilies appear in the Aalsmeer auction rooms, together with a wonderful array of cyclamens and miniature azaleas, both popular as Christmas presents.

And in September when the town goes all out for its Bloemencorso or flower festival, something over two million blossoms are used for the huge decorated floats, a sight that attracts thousands of flower fanciers to Amsterdam's Olympic stadium.

Holland's Bulbfields

Still dazzled by the sight of so many flowers in one place, we retrace our route for half a kilometer or so to the edge of the Haarlemmermeer Polder, where we plunge west across its middle on a road so straight that, before we realize it, we are through Hoofddorp or "Head Village," a burgeoning town of 40,000 inhabitants, many of whom work at Schiphol. On the far side of the polder, just as the road climbs slightly to go over the western dike, a strange building on the right attracts our eye.

This is the Cruquius Pumping Station, one of three steam-powered stations that pumped out the Haarlemmermeer Polder. It was in continuous use until 1933, when it was converted into the Museum de Cruquius that well merits a stop. Besides explaining by means of working models how a polder drainage system works, it contains a relief map of the entire Netherlands which can be flooded at will and then pumped dry in a vivid demonstration of the fate that would overtake the country if all the dikes were to give way (producing a rise in sea level calculated at 49 meters, or 160 feet!). Models of various kinds of windmills can be seen here as well as an explanation of how major dikes are constructed today. Don't overlook the Cruquius pump, an engineering giant with eight beams transmitting power to as many pumps from a single cylinder with 3-meter (10-foot) stroke. The pumps had a capacity of 386,400 liters (85,000 gallons) per minute and operated for 84 years.

The delightful garden city of Heemstede lies on the higher ground just outside the Haarlemmermeer. If the bulb season is past, we continue west to Zandvoort. Let's assume, however, that it's April or early May and turn south for Bennebroek and the most important bulbfields.

Such great progress has been made in producing new varieties of the main bulb plants that the calendar is no longer quite the tyrant it used to be. Still, there is a general progression in this part of Holland from daffodils and narcissi from the end of March to the middle of April, early tulips and hyacinths from the second week of April to the end of the month, and late tulips immediately afterwards. An early or late spring can move these approximate dates forward or backward by as much as three weeks.

The art of bulb-growing, by the way, has been a Dutch specialty since the first tulip was brought to Holland from Turkey in 1559. In 1625 an offer of 3,000 florins for two bulbs was turned down, but the speculation in bulbs became a mania during the years 1634–1637, as irrational and popular as stock market speculation in the late 1920's, when fortunes were made—and lost—in a single day. Individual bulbs worth thousands of guilders had their pictures painted in tulip books that enjoyed a similar vogue. Only during the last 60 years has the scientific approach prevailed. Today's experts diagnose the rarest tulips illustrated in the books that have survived as suffering from viruses that caused abnormal (and beautiful) coloring or shape.

The bulbfields themselves extend from just north of Leiden to the southern limits of Haarlem, but the greatest concentration is limited to the district that begins at Sassenheim and ends between Hillegom and Bennebroek. In a neat checkerboard pattern of brilliant color the fields stretch out as far as the eye can see.

The apparent artificiality of the sharply defined rectangular fields is not a concession to taste. It is part of the businesslike efficiency of an industry that has made the bulb one of Holland's most important export commodities. It must be remembered that here the bulb, not the flower, is the most important part of the plant. When the flowers bloom, the heads are cut off, leaving only the green stalks. The children play with the discarded blooms, threading them into garlands which they sell to passing motorists or use to make floral mosaics.

Let's follow the main Hillegom-Lisse-Sassenheim road south from Heemstede. This is the core of the bulb-growing district. Along the road you may notice flower mosaics on one side or the other. These are worked out, petal by petal, by the local residents in competition with each other, usually reaching their peak just before the annual Bloemencorso or flower parade. Held on a Saturday during late April, this procession is a highlight of the year in this part of Holland. Dozens of magnificent floats, covered with multicolored blooms, are prepared and put on display, first in Lisse. The main procession, accompanied by marching bands, starts in Haarlem and covers a 10 km. (6 mile) route through Bennebroek, Hillegom, Lisse, Sassenheim and Nordwijkerhout to Noordwijk, by which time it is evening and the floats are illuminated. They remain on show for the rest of the weekend at the Koningin Wilhelmina Boulevard in Noordwijk.

Keukenhof Gardens

Lisse, the middle of the three main bulb towns, is noted for its Keukenhof Gardens, but we keep straight ahead to Sassenheim, turning right (west) into the bulbfields at the north edge of town. At Loosterweg we head north again, following the zigs and zags of this country lane as it passes through the very heart of the fields so overburdened with color. Presently we are back at Lisse again, and follow the signs for Keukenhof. In Lisse, at 219 Heereweg, is a museum devoted to the history and cultivation of bulbs.

From the end of March to late May the 28-hectare (70-acre) Keukenhof Gardens, founded by leading bulb-growers, are a living open-air flower exhibition that is unique in the world. As many as 5–6 million bulbs blossom here together, either in the 5000 sq. meters of hothouses or in flower-beds along the sides of a charming lake. Holland's leading bulb-growers have joined together to make this old estate a permanent treasure house of floral beauty. Set in a park dotted with lakes, the world's largest flower show draws huge crowds to its regimental lines of tulips, hyacinths, and daffodils. It is open from late March to late May, daily from 8 A.M. to 7.30 P.M. Admission is Fl. 15. Telephone 02521–19034 for more information. A lazier way to see the flowers is from the windows of the Leiden–Haarlem train.

Here you can always spot the lively "meisjes" (girls) selling guidebooks. The girls' costumes date from the lifetime of Jacoba van Beieren, who had her hunting lodge here in the 15th century, and who was in succession Dauphiness of France, Duchess of Gloucester and Countess of Bavaria.

Spring is not the only time of the year when this man-made tide of color bursts the dikes and floods the fields around Lisse. Just as the many hues of hyacinths and tulips march across the countryside in disciplined ranks during April and May, so in July and August do the stately gladioli welcome visitors to this domain. Then, in September, the dahlia takes over by way of emphasizing the horticultural preeminence of these sandy fields by the North Sea. A further Lisse attraction is the Huys Dever, a keep dating from 1375 and providing a setting for exhibitions and concerts.

From Keukenhof, Loosterweg III leads to North Holland and to Vogelenzang, which name means birds' song. Birds there are, too, in profusion, for this is the wooded edge of the dunes that next lead us due west to the cosmopolitan seaside resort of Zandvoort. Just north of Vogelenzang you can visit the nursery of a leading bulb grower, Frans Roozen, with exquisite gardens, greenhouses and fields of blooms. Up to 1,000 varieties are grown here. Open daily from 8–6 during April and May for the tulip show, and from July through September open Monday through Friday, 9–5, for summer flowers. Entrance is free.

At Zandvoort is the 5-km. (3-mile), closed circuit for motorcycles and cars where races are held. The coastal road turns abruptly inland a mile or so beyond the entrance to the Zandvoort track, leading us back through dunes to Bloemendaal, a charming town, whose open-air theater hosts some 40 performances a year. In addition, it offers a miniature lake and botanical gardens.

Along the coast, within easy reach of Lisse, are a number of beach resorts, large and small. The best known, in addition to Zandvoort, are Noordwijk and Katwijk.

Haarlem, Home of the Arts

In the heart of Haarlem we find the earliest center of Dutch art. A delightful stop in this 746-year-old city of 154,000 people is the Frans Halsmuseum housing a fine collection of masterpieces by this famous Dutch painter and other artists who worked here in the 16th and 17th centuries. The building, 62 Groot Heiligland, in which the display is presented, was originally part of the Oudemannenhuis, a former senior citizens' home for men built in 1608 by Ghent architect Lieven de Key (1560–1627). The building, an arcade of rooms around a central courtyard, is magnificently preserved. Contemporary art is displayed in a new wing (1985). Concerts are presented on the third Sunday of the month.

Several blocks away, the landmark Grote Kerk is girdled with souvenir shops literally growing out of its walls and buttresses. The interior as well as the outside of this imposing structure reveal to the trained eye the architecture of three centuries. Consecrated in 1519, it took more than 100 years to build. Above all, look at the organ, one of Europe's most famous, with three keyboards, 68 registers, and 5,000 pipes. Built in 1738 by C. Mueller, it has been played on by Mozart and Händel, and many more modern masters of that form of music. Organ recitals are given on Tuesdays and Thursdays in July and August and there are important international organ music festivals held annually in early July. Over recent years it has been extensively restored and is open to visitors.

The genius of Frans Hals (c.1580–1666) has not only established itself in his peerless paintings, but has also influenced such painters as Buytewech, Terborch and Brouwer. Hals is one of the finest portrait painters that Holland has ever produced, and his corporation pieces, paintings of the guilds of Haarlem, are to be admired in the museum. The setting for these arresting paintings, some amazingly virile and some unbelievably peaceful, is in itself a gem of artistry.

In the center of Haarlem, around the large market square (Grote Markt), the whole story of Dutch architecture can be traced in a chain of majestic buildings ranging through the 15th, 16th, 17th, 18th, and 19th centuries. With a smile and perhaps a little bravado you can enter most of them, from the Town Hall, originally the 14th-century hunting lodge of the counts of Holland, with its candle-lit and tapestried Council Chamber, to the Meat Market, of all places, one of Holland's greatest Renaissance buildings of the beginning of the 17th century. Today, it often houses the most adventurous of modern art exhibitions and is part of the Frans Hals Museum, known as *De Hallen*. Since the canvases in this sinister building are lit by natural light, try to see the museum on a sunny day. As you leave, glance at the graceful wooden bridge over the Spaarne.

With its secret inner courtyards, pointed gables and spiritually enclosed almshouses, Haarlem can resemble a 17th-century canvas, even one painted by Frans Hals, the city's greatest painter. Some of the facades on the market square are adorned with such homilies as "The body's sickness is a cure for the soul."

Housed in its remarkable collection of architecture, Haarlem offers a variety of museums. In the Teylers Museum, Holland's first museum, besides a fine collection of the Hague school of painting, you can see an unexpected collection of original sketches and drawings by Michelangelo, Raphael and other non-Dutch masters, against a background of fossils and other petrified remains.

Of more recent date is the impressive Saint Bavo Basilica, designed by Cuypers and built between 1895 and 1906, with the towers completed in 1930. The red brick building is a complex of fanciful towers and roofs, on a considerable scale. Over 100 meters long and 60 meters high it has beautiful stained glass windows, sculptures and pictures and is open Monday to Saturday from April to September 10–12 and 2–4.30. Organ concerts are held here each Saturday at 6 P.M. The Corrie ten Boomhuis, a museum since 1985, is a testimonial to the courage and endurance of the Dutch, who sheltered their neighbors during World War II, at great risk to their own lives.

Each Saturday during the blooming season there is a colorful flower market in Grote Markt, and every year on one Saturday during April a spectacular flower parade between Haarlem and Noordwijk. As a summer break from Haarlem's daunting museums, Zandvoort's sandy beaches can be very alluring. Adventurous visitors prefer Zandvoort's casino or two-mile long nudist beach. There are regular bus services to Zandvoort in the summer. (For information, contact the VVV; tel. 02507–17947.)

Spaarndam's Statue to a Legend

A couple of kilometers or so northeast of Haarlem is a statue to a legend, a statue that proves once again the power of imaginative fiction. You may recall the young boy Pieter who appears in the pages of an American book called *Hans Brinker or the Silver Skates.* The story goes that he discovered a hole in a dike one afternoon and plugged it with his finger while waiting for help to come. All night long he stood vigil until, when help finally arrived the following morning, he was dead, having heroically saved Haarlem from destruction.

So many people have asked where Pieter lived and where he performed his brave deed that the Dutch finally felt compelled to do something about the legend. In 1950 Princess Irene, accompanied by her mother Queen Juliana, unveiled a memorial, if not to Pieter, then to the courage and devotion of Dutch youth through the centuries. The place selected was Spaarndam, a choice as logical as any and more picturesque than most. Even if no dike could be saved by so puny an instrument as a boy's finger, the memorial has been cunningly placed so that the motorist who stops to admire it can plug the flow of traffic around with 100% effectiveness. Needless to say, most Dutch people, when asked, know nothing whatever about the legend. It is one of those happy fictions that has the ring of truth.

Following the signs for Zwanenburg, we rejoin the main Haarlem-Amsterdam highway, and are back in the city of canals in 30 minutes.

IV—AMSTERDAM SOUTHEAST TO MUIDEN, NAARDEN AND HILVERSUM

The last of our four Amsterdam-based trips takes us along the southern edge of the IJsselmeer to the garden district of Gooiland, a 120-km. (75-mile) excursion that reaches into what is technically Utrecht Province long enough to see the Queen Mother's palace at Soestdijk, Queen Beatrix' palace of Drakenstein at Lage Vuursche where she lived until she moved to Den Haag after her Coronation, and the villages of Spakenburg and Bunschoten, and the pleasant woodland town of Baarn.

First stop is Muiden, 18 km. (11 miles) east of Amsterdam, whose castle, Muiderslot, stands on the right (east) bank of the Vecht River at its confluence with the IJsselmeer. As early as the beginning of the 10th century, a wooden tollhouse was erected on this site. Gradually it was rebuilt and enlarged. The castle, a red brick building, became a fortress after 1205 to guard the banks of the Vecht, and was reconstructed by Count Floris V of Holland who was assassinated here by noblemen in 1296. From 1621 the Muiderslot was the meeting place of a circle of poets and intellectuals led by P. C. Hooft (1581–1647), and brought together celebrities like Vondel, Grotius and Maria Tesselschade. This group became known as the

Muiderkring. After Hooft's death, the castle was neglected, but in 1948 its interior was restored to the state of Hooft's day. A half hour spent exploring its galleries and enjoying the view of the IJsselmeer is well spent, especially in view of the fact that Holland has relatively few such relics of sterner times.

About 6 km. (4 miles) farther east is Naarden, a fortified town of 19,000 souls whose star-shaped earthen ramparts and moats have been miraculously preserved despite a succession of bloody sieges and massacres. Here the dreaded Spanish Duke of Alva refined the art of torture; and in 1572 burned the town to the ground. One hundred years later, the French broke through the town's defenses. In comparison with other European walled cities it seems more like a toy fort, although observed from the air it shows correctness of design and stern obedience to the principles of self-protection. An intriguing military museum is inside the fortifications, and soldiers in costume fire the antique weapons on the third Sunday each month in summer. The 17th-century Bohemian pedagogue Comenius lived and died here (a special chapel perpetuates his memory) and the 1601 Dutch Renaissance Town Hall is charming inside. Thanks to outstanding acoustics, the 15th-century church is the locale for an annual performance of Bach's St. Matthew Passion.

Bussum, practically next door, wears a more modern aspect. So much so, in fact, that Holland's first television studios were established here amid the comfortable homes, wide boulevards, and public buildings.

Beyond Bussum we enter Gooiland, a region of lakes and woods whose scenic beauty has attracted the well-to-do from Amsterdam and elsewhere. Just 6 km. (4 miles) farther along is Laren, famous as an artists' colony. About the turn of the century, artists of Den Haag School, attracted by the paintability of the district, congregated here and formed a group known as the luministen. Others joined them until today there are over a hundred modern painters and sculptors living in the neighborhood whose works are displayed from time to time in the Singer Museum with its collection of paintings and engravings by the American artist William Singer, Jr. In October there is a major flower display, *Herstflora,* to celebrate the harvest.

Baarn (in the province of Utrecht), another town of the wealthy, lies just south of the road we take to the still traditional towns of Bunschoten and Spakenburg, the latter with a fine IJsselmeer harbor. Costumes here have practically died out, though some villagers wear them on summer Wednesdays for the tourists. The distinctive feature of the women's clothing here is the Kraplap, made of brightly flowered cotton, shaped like a cuirassier's breastplate and starched to about the same rigidity, a holdover from medieval garb. For a good look, stop by the Museum of Traditional Clothing and Fishing, behind the Noorderkerk.

Retracing our tracks to Baarn, we turn south with Soestdijk as our goal. A vaguely semicircular building by the side of the highway is the palace of the Queen Mother, now *Princess* Juliana, and Prince Bernhard, who may emerge with no fanfare in their own car.

Heading back towards Baarn a third time, we swing west along the Hilversum road, which runs past the Hooge Vuursche castle hotel.

Hilversum up the Vecht to Breukelen

Hilversum has two claims to distinction: it is the home of Dutch radio and TV broadcasting, and renowned for the outstanding modern architecture designed by Dudok. Although broadcasting is a state monopoly in the Netherlands with the government imposing a monthly license fee, the six stations are under Catholic, Protestant, Socialist, and independent management. Their studios, the schools, the public baths, and most particularly the angular Town Hall are among the outstanding examples of the architect's art.

Emerging on the west side of Hilversum we follow the road to Loenen, presently crossing the middle of the popular Loosdrecht Lakes, one of the most attractive swimming and yachting centers in the Netherlands. Loenen itself graces the west bank of the Vecht River, whose outlet into the IJsselmeer we saw during our visit to the castle at Muiden. The district from here south along the river to Breukelen and Maarssen enjoyed a great vogue during the second half of the 17th and the first half of the 18th century among prosperous Amsterdam merchants who built country houses beside the water in a style already showing signs of decadence, an abandonment of the austere classical line in favor of French influences. Many of these homes have been restored during recent years by wealthy Amsterdammers and foundations that use the buildings as headquarters, and if the result is hardly Dutch, the effect is nonetheless delightful as the road winds and twists around each bend of the Vecht. These old patrician houses are best seen by taking a boat trip on the river, or by bike or car along the banks. Boats leave from the center of Utrecht for cruises up the Vecht, with a two-hour lunch stop in Loenen.

We continue as far as Breukelen in the province of Utrecht, or possibly half a kilometer beyond to the 13th-century Castle of Nijenrode, on the right-hand side of the road, today a training school for Dutch executives. Breukelen itself is just another sleepy town drowsing by the river bank, but Americans may be startled to learn that it gave its name to Brooklyn, which still retains memories of the Dutch who founded it. On the water side of the village is the Breukelen bridge, rather more modest than its famous counterpart, since the river is no more than 6 meters (20 feet) wide at this point.

From Breukelen a 2 km. (1 mile) link to the west brings us to the express highway that runs from Utrecht north to Amsterdam, a distance, from this point, of only 25 km. (16 miles). So enchanting is the Vecht district, however, that you may prefer to follow the river to Loenen once again before turning west for the highway back to our starting point.

This is a delightful region to sample the country hotels, often in old buildings in charming surroundings.

MOTORING AROUND THE IJSSELMEER

Although it's possible to drive around the IJsselmeer in a single day, you are advised to allow at least two days for the journey. If you can spare three or four days, include one or two other stops en route.

Two-Day Itinerary

Amsterdam north to Volendam (brief pause), Edam (visit Kaaswaag museum), Hoorn (visit De Waag or Weigh House in central square, also harbor), Enkhuizen (visit Zuiderzee museums) for late lunch, then via Hoogkarspel and Wervershoof to Medemblik (brief pause) and Den Oever where the enclosing dike begins. In the middle, at Breezanddijk, is a monument with a tower that affords an outstanding view, where you can stop for tea or coffee. At the north end of the dike, turn south at Schettens, and follow signs to Makkum for a brief stop at the porcelain factory; then on to Workum, Hindeloopen. Pause here for a walk through this canal-laced town. Back on the road, bypass Staveren and head for Koudum, Rijs, Sondel, and Lemmer, where a fast road takes you across the Noordoost-polder to Emmeloord. There are few, and mostly small, hotels in these country towns and the best bets for overnight accommodations are Bols-ward, Sneek or Emmeloord.

From Emmeloord, take the small road to Urk (best chance for parking is by the harbor) for costumes and a breath of the IJsselmeer, before continuing east to Ens with a brief pause at Schokland to see the island and its minuscule museum. Continue southeast to Kampen, then swing south-west to the medieval facades of Elburg. Nunspeet and Hierden are next along the secondary road, which runs just north of the motorway. Drive slowly for a glimpse of local costumes. At Harderwijk, drive north along the dike as far as the Hardersluis (locks) for an impression of Holland's newest polder, then back to Harderwijk and on to the colorful villages of Bunschoten and Spakenburg via Putten and Nijkerk. After a stop to sample Spakenburg, you return to Amsterdam by the main highway, detouring briefly at Naarden and Muiden.

This makes a very full two days and assumes two early starts.

Three-Day Itinerary

The first day is the same as the Two-Day Itinerary above, stopping overnight at Emmeloord, or Sneek.

In the morning you visit Urk and Schokland, as above, but instead of turning south at Ens you continue east to Vollenhove and St. Jansklooster, where you take the causeway across the delightful Beulaker Wijde to the crossroads De Blauwe Hand, turning left (north) from there for Giet-hoorn, a now very touristy village that has canals and footpaths instead of streets. After a half-hour visit here, you continue east to Meppel, then swing south and turn off the main highway to drive through the costume villages of Staphorst (being sure not to take any pictures of the pious people who live there without their express permission) and Rouveen Zwolle is next (brief visit), followed by medieval Elburg (visit as on Two-Day Itin-erary) and Harderwijk, via Nunspeet and Hierden.

The trip out to Lelystad and a visit to the Nieuwland Information Center is interesting because of the impression you gain of what is involved in reclaiming land on so vast a scale. A visit to the replica of the 17th-century ship under construction next door to the center is also of interest.

The morning of the third day, cut east and slightly south to the villages of Lage Vuursche and Soestdijk for a glimpse of, respectively, Drakestein and Soestdijk palaces. Then swing over to Baarn and northwest through Laren to Naarden. Turn south once more to Hilversum, cut west across the pleasant Loosdrecht Lakes to Loenen, on the banks of the delightful Vecht River, lined with 17th-century country houses built by wealthy Amsterdammers. Turn south to Breukelen, which gave its name to New York City's famous borough.

From Breukelen follow the express highway back to Amsterdam if it's late in the day. If not, cross the Breukelen bridge and follow the Vecht north to Loenerslot. At the N201, continue on to Vreeland, Kortenhoef, and the A1 at Laren. If time permits, stop at Muiden for tea at the castle before returning to Amsterdam. Since the creation of the Bijlmermeer suburb of Amsterdam and new expressways, the smaller roads have been rerouted, so follow the signposts carefully, but it is worth the effort as the drive is so much more interesting.

Four-Day Itinerary

This is an elaboration of the above. Allow yourself more time to explore Hoorn, Enkhuizen, and Medemblik, then cross the enclosing dike and spend the night in charming Sneek, or in Bolsward.

The next morning, head north for Leeuwarden (visit), west to Franeker (visit), then south to Schettens, where the route into Emmeloord is the same as for the previous two itineraries.

The third and fourth days are the same as the second and third days of the Three-Day Itinerary.

In this tour you would be well advised to plan to spend an hour or so at the Dolphinarium at Harderwijk. This is an enthralling experience, because not only do the dolphins put up a remarkable circus performance but the directors also run a dolphin research station studying the habits and language of these delightful creatures. It is open daily from March to October.

Not very far from Harderwijk is the Flevohof Park, a remarkable composite "working" exhibition of everything agricultural and horticultural in Holland. It gives the visitor a day on a farm, with every form of visual display, and there is a host of fun entertainment for the children, water sports, etc. Open daily from April to October. A sidetrip out of Harderwijk, 32 km. to the north, is to Lelystad, where one can visit the Nieuwland Information Center, with remains of ship wrecks recovered from the reclaimed Zuiderzee. Be sure to visit the 17th-century sailing ship, the *Batavia,* at the boat yard next door.

Instead of returning to Amsterdam at the end of any of these tours, you can easily leave the shores of the IJsselmeer at Hilversum and turn south for Den Haag via either Utrecht, Woerden, Alphen aan de Rijn, and Leiden, or (more direct and much faster) Utrecht and thence by the express highway straight to Den Haag, with a brief stop in Gouda.

PRACTICAL INFORMATION FOR
THE AMSTERDAM REGION

WHEN TO GO. The best time to visit its surroundings is from mid-**April** to the end of **September,** with **July** and **August** being the peak months to avoid. Because of the bulbfields, the first week of May is possibly the best moment of all if flowers are high on your list of things to see. If spring comes early, however, the peak of the tulips, hyacinths, and narcissi can be as early as the first week of April, with nothing but heaps of discarded blooms left in the fields a fortnight later. The annual Bloemencorso or Flower Parade through the bulbfields takes place on a Saturday during April, running from Haarlem to Nordwijk.

Because the bulbfields are such an unpredictable factor, they should not be given too much weight in the scheduling of your trip, especially if it is to be a brief one. There will still be plenty of flowers to see in May no matter what. Here are some of the other attractions:

The Keukenhof Gardens always open in late **March** nowadays and can be visited until late May, from 8 A.M. to 7.30 P.M. The last Friday in **April** is the traditional beginning date of the sprightly Alkmaar cheese market, which continues every Friday morning until late September. **May 4** is Memorial Day. From mid-June to mid-August Hoorn stages a folklore market every Wednesday, while Schagen holds a West Frisian folklore market every Thursday. Haarlem is the site of the International Organ Competitions in early **July.** During the first two weeks in **August** international sailing regattas are staged at Loosdrecht, Muiden and Medemblik. In early **September,** Aalsmeer stages its annual flower parade, to Amsterdam and back. Holland's Sinterklaas (St. Nickola) comes to town in various cities mid-**November.**

TELEPHONE CODES. We have given telephone codes for all the towns and villages in this chapter in the hotel and restaurant listings that follow. These codes need only be used when calling from outside the town or village concerned.

HOTELS AND RESTAURANTS. Because few tourists consider staying anywhere else but Amsterdam or Den Haag when they visit this corner of the Netherlands, hotel accommodations are relatively simple (with the notable exception of Hilversum). Moreover, most of the towns are so small that gourmet restaurants are also scarce. If you are a little adventurous, however, and willing to put up with quarters that are spotlessly clean, if simple, then there is no reason why you should feel bound to Amsterdam. Your reward will be a more leisurely pace through the countryside, the opportunity to come in closer contact with the Dutch, and noticeably lower hotel and restaurant costs.

In many instances, the restaurant of the leading hotel may be the best place to stop for a meal. If so, no restaurant recommendations are made in the listing that follows. If you see *paling* (eel) on the menu, remember that it's often a specialty of the house. If you have your doubts, at least try the smoked variety as an appetizer on a piece of toast.

We have divided the hotels and restaurants in our listings into three categories—Expensive (E), Moderate (M) and Inexpensive (I). We give prices for hotels and restaurants in *Facts at Your Fingertips.* Most hotels, particularly at the upper end of the scale, have rooms in more than one category and a consequently wide range of prices. Outside big cities, the room price normally includes breakfast. Remember, too, that many restaurants have dishes in more than one category, so be sure to check the menu outside *before* you go in. Look out too for the excellent value Tourist Menu.

Figures in brackets after place names are mileage from Amsterdam.

Alkmaar (22 northwest). Site of Holland's most interesting cheese market. *Alkmaar Comfort Inn* (M), 2 Arcadialaan; 072–401414. *Markzicht* (M), 34 Houttil overlooks Friday market, 072–113283. *De Nachtegaal* (M), 100 Langestraat; 072–112894. Tourist menu offered. *Ida Magaretha* (I), 186 Kanaaldijk 4 km. outside town center, 072–613989.

Restaurants. Hotels *Marktzicht* and *De Nachtegaal* both have good restaurants. *Le Bistrot de Paris* (E), 1 Waagplein; 072–120023. French, centrally located near Weigh House. *Rôtisserie Rue du Bois* (E), 3e van den Boschstraat; 072–119733. Tourist menu. Separate bar and terrace. *Koekenbier* (M), 16 Kennemerstraatweg; 072–114386. Excellent Scandinavian buffet on Saturday. *Deli* (I), 8 Munt; 072–154082. An Indonesian restaurant in a 17th-century house. *'t Gulden Vlies (I),* 30 Koorstraat; 072–122442.

Baarn (23 southwest). *De Hooge Vuursche* (E), 14 Hilversumsestraadweg; 02154–12541. 27 rooms with bath. Luxurious castle-hotel on the road to Hilversum. Extensive grounds, terraces, fountains. *Royal* (M), 21 Hoofdstraat; 02154–129661. 12 rooms.

Badhoevedorp. *Dorint Hotel Schiphol Amsterdam* (E), 299 Sloterweg; 06–099–5599. This brand-new 201-room hotel has many amenities (9 indoor tennis and 5 indoor squash courts, pool, and fitness center), plus two restaurants, bar and a shuttle service to nearby Schiphol airport.

Bennebroek (14 southwest). **Restaurant.** *Les Jumeaux* (M–E), 19b Bennebroekerlaan; 02502–46334. Favored by families, this restaurant is operated by twin brothers who feature both classical and modern French cuisine. Dining in the indoor/outdoor garden with an electrically operated roof is a special treat in any season.

Bergen (26 northwest). Once famous for its artists' colony. *Elzenhof* (M), 78 Dorpstraat; 02208–12401. 30 rooms, sauna, whirlpool. Modest prices for quality. *Marijke* (M), 23 Dorpstraat; 02208–12381. 90 rooms, some in renovated annex. Inexpensive for quality. *Zee-Bergen* (M), 11 Wilhelminalaan; 02208–97241. 21 rooms, garden. One of the best.

Bergen aan Zee (3 west of Bergen). Quiet family seaside resort. *Nassau-Bergen* (E), 4 Van der Wijckplein; 02208–97541. 42 rooms, most with bath; sauna, solarium; near the beach. Closed Dec.-Jan. *Prins Maurits* (M),

7 van Hasseltweg; 02208–12364. 25 rooms mostly with bath. Near the beach and forest. *De Stormvogel* (I), 12 Jac. Kalffweg; 02208–12734. 11 rooms, near beach.

Bloemendaal (13 west). A garden suburb of Haarlem, 3 miles from the sea. *Iepenhove* (M), 4 Hartenlustlaan; 023–258301. 40 rooms, some with bath, in residential area, just off main street. *Rusthoek* (I), 141 Bloemendaalseweg; 023–257050. 22 rooms, 10 with bath; restaurant.

Restaurant. *Bokkodoorns* (E), 53 Zeeweg; 023–263600. First class French novelle cuisine. Recommended. Closed Sat. lunch and Mon.

Bovenkarspel (67 northeast). *Het Rode Hert* (M), 235 Hoofstraat; 02285–11412. Romantically housed in a 16th-century inn.

Restaurant. *De Halve Maan* (M), 254 Hoofstraat; 02285–52251. Nederlands Dis menu.

Bussum (16 east). On edge of the charming Gooiland district. *Golden Tulip Hotel Jan Tabak* (E), 27 Amersfoortsestraatweg; 02159–59911. 100 good modern rooms. Pool, gardens with tennis. 30 mins. from Schiphol. *Gooiland* (M), 16 Stationsweg; 02159–43724. 24 comfortable rooms. *Hotel Cecil* (M), 25 Brinklaan.

Restaurant. *Auberge Maître Pierre* (E), 16 Stationsweg. On the pricey side, but worth it.

Callantsoog (39 northwest). Small, seaside family resort. *Callantsoog* (M), 26 Abbestederweg; 02248–2222. 65 brand-new rooms; pool, indoor tennis, squash, near beach, restaurant. *De Wijde Blick* (M), 2 Zeeweg; 02248–1317. Small, with a good restaurant.

Castricum (20 northwest). Quiet town on edge of the dunes, 3 miles from the beach. *Kornman* (I), 1 Mient; 02518–52251. 10 rooms, some with bath.

Restaurant. *'t Eethuisje* (M), 53 Dorpsstraat; 02518–52043.

Den Helder (48 north). Important naval base and ferry terminus for island of Texel. *Beatrix* (E), 2 Badhuisstraat; 02230–14800. 40 rooms, excellent, full fitness center including squash. *Hotel Forest* (M), 43 Julianaplein; 02230–14858. 30 rooms. *Motel den Helder* (M), 2 Marsdiepstraat; 02230–22333. 75 rooms. *Wienerhof* (I), 7 Parallelweg; 02230–16895. 14 rooms and restaurant.

Den Oever (45 north). Southern terminus of the enclosing dike that leads to Friesland. *Zomerdijk* (M), 65 Zwinstraat; 02271–1404. 14 rooms. *De Haan* (I), 4 Oeverdijk; 02271–1205. 5 rooms with a good restaurant. *Wiron* (I), 20–24 Voorstraat; 02271–1255. 17 rooms.

Edam (14 northeast). *Fortuna* (M), 8 Spuistraat; 02993–71671. 30 rooms and cosy. *Damhotel* (I), 1 Keizersgracht; 02293–71766.

Egmond aan Zee (25 northwest). Seaside resort. *Bellevue* (E), A-7 Boulevard; 02206–1025. 50 rooms near the beach. Excellent package arrangements, French restaurant. *Golfzang* (M), 19 Blvd Ir. de Vassy;

02206–1516. 20 rooms. *Sunny Home* (M), Ir. Paralleleweg 2–4, 02206–1368. Family hotel in the center of town. Tourist menu offered. *Sonnevanck* (I), 114–116 Wilhelminastraat; 02206–1589. 16 rooms, restaurant, 100 yards from beach.

Emmeloord. *t'Voorhuys* (M), 20 De Deel; 05270–12441. Modern rooms and facilities with reasonable restaurant. City center.

Enkhuizen (35 northeast). Attractive old walled city. *Het Wapen van Enkhuizen* (M), 59 Breedstraat; 02280–13434. 20 rooms, about half with bath or shower. Tourist menu. *Die Port van Cleve* (M), 74 Dijk; 02280–12510. 20 rooms, near the old harbor. Tourist menu and Nederlands Dis menu. *Du Passage* (M), 8 Paktuinen; 02280–12462. Small (24 rooms) with good restaurant.

Restaurant. *Die Drie Haringhe* (M), 28 Dijk; 02280–18610. French cuisine in an old warehouse overlooking the waterfront; there is a secluded cellar bar for windy days! Try the *lekkerkje* (fried fish) or the *maatjes haring* (raw herring).

Haarlem (12 west). *Lion d'Or* (E), 34 Kruisweg; 023–321750. 40 rooms. Situated just five minutes from the old city center, this comfortable hotel offers various packages, including golf. Gourmet evening meals. *Carillon* (M), 27 Grote Markt; 023–310591. 11 rooms. Central. Old-style Dutch restaurant.

Restaurants. *Bokkedorens* (E), 53 Zeeweg, Overveen; 023–263600. Star-classed restaurant among the dunes. Closed Mon. *Le Chat Noir* (E), 1 Bakkumstraat; 023–317387. French and worth the price. *Peter Cuyper* (M–E), 70 Kleine Houtstraat; 023–320885. Try the lamb and fish. Closed Sun. *De Componist* (M), 1 Korte Veerstraat; 023–32885. The long time and extremely popular restaurant features beef with its own secret herb sauce. *Los Gauchos* (M), 9 Kruisstraat; 023–320358. One of a chain of Argentine steak houses. *De Gekroonde Hamer* (I–M), 24 Breestraat; 023–312243. Fish and vegetarian dishes are favorites at this place, where roof-garden dining is also a big attraction. *De Karmeliet* (I), 6 Spekstraat; 023–314426.

Heemskerk. *Hotel Chateau Marquette* (E), 34 Marquettelaan; 02510–41414. 88 rooms in modern hotel on castle grounds, with bar, restaurant, meeting rooms, and library in castle. A shuttle bus travels between the castle and hotel.

Hilversum (20 southeast). *Het Hof van Holland* (M), 1–7 Kerksbrink; 035–246141. 55 rooms with bath; restaurant. *Hilfertsom* (M), 28 Koninginneweg; 035–232444. 44 rooms, most with bath.

Restaurants. *Het Zwarte Paard* (M), la Larenseweg. *Me Chow Low* (M), 25 Groest. *Palace Residence* (M), 86 s' Gravelandseweg. *Rôtisserie Napoléon* (M), in the Hotel de Nederlanden at nearby Vreeland. A local favorite.

Hoorn (25 north). Historic seaport. *De Keizerskroon* (M), 31–33 Breed; 02290–12717. The oldest in town. *Petit Noord* (M), 53 Kleine Noord; 02290–12750. 34 rooms, all with bath; pleasant restaurant.

Restaurants. *De Oude Rosmolen* (E), 1 Duinsteeg; 02290–14752. Building dates from 1635. French cuisine, superb quality. Closed Tues. and Thurs. *Rijk van Wijk* (E), 1 Vismarkt; 02290–16483. French cuisine, reservation necessary. Closed Mon. and Tues. *De Waag* (M), 8 Roode Steen; 02290–15195. Fish specialties and French cuisine. Antique room, terrace. *Bontekoe Taverne* (M) 1 Nieuwendam; 02290–17324. Traditional family restaurant with French-Dutch cuisine.

IJmuiden (16 northwest). Gateway to the North Sea Canal, 1 block from Europe's biggest locks. *Augusta* (I), 98 Oranjestraaat; 02550–14217. 14 rooms with shower. Simple, but comfortable.

Katwoude, near Volendam (see below). *Katwoude Motel* (E), 1 Wagenweg; 02993–65656. 86 rooms; reasonable restaurant, swimming pool, sauna.

Laren (18 southeast). Artists' colony just outside Hilversum. *De Witte Bergen* (M), 02738–86754. 60 rooms with shower. *Herberg t'Langenbaergh* (M), 1 Deventerweg; 02153–1209. 10 rooms.
Restaurants. *Auberge La Provence* (E), 2 Westherheide; 02153–87974. Excellent French restaurant with superb sea food. Closed for Sat. and Sun. lunch. *Coeswaard* (I), 18a Brink, opposite church, 02153–83462. Famed for Dutch pancakes.

Maarssen (10 southeast). *De Nonnerie* (M), 51 Lange Gracht; 03465–62201. 16 rooms; restaurant closed in Feb.
Restaurant. *Wilgenplas* (M), Maarssenseveenvaart 7a, just out of town. 03465–61590. Excellent food.

Medemblik (64 north). *Het Wapen van Medemblik* (M), 1 Oosterhaven; 02274–3844. 28 rooms. Tourist menus; good quality for the price.
Restaurant. *Twee Schouwtjes* (M), 27 Oosterhaven; 02274–1956. Good restaurant in 17th-century house. Open hearth in winter. By the harbor.

Monnickendam. *De Posthoorn* (M), 43 Noordeinde; 02995–1471. An excellent fish restaurant. *De Waegh* (M), Haven; 02995–1241. Small and delightful pancake restaurant overlooking a canal near the harbor. *Nieuw Stuttenburgh* (I), 4 Haringburgwal; 02995–1398. Antique musical instruments add to the decor. Try the *Monnickendammer twalf uurtje,* a dish of three smoked fish.

Naarden. *Days Inn* (M), 3 IJsselmeerweg; 02159–51514 or 800–325–2325 in U.S. The first of its kind in the Netherlands, this U.S.-style lakeside hotel is conveniently just off Highway A1. All 70 rooms with bath, color T.V., and video. À-la-carte restaurant.

Ouderkerk (4 south). Rapidly growing village on the Amstel river. *t'Jagerhuis* (M), 4 Amstelzijde; 02963–1432. 25 rooms; closed Dec. and Jan.
Restaurant. *Klein Paardenburg* (E), 59 Amstelzijde; 02963–1335. Small award-winning restaurant.

Sassenheim (10 south of Haarlem). *Motel Sassenheim* (M), 8 Warmonderweg; 02522–19019. 70 rooms with bath; recommended.

Schagen (38 northwest). *de Roode Leeuw* (I), 15 Markt; 02240–12537. 13 rooms, some with bath, in center.

Texel Island (60 north). Reached by ferry from Den Helder; most hotels close during the winter. At **De Koog,** on Texel's west shore: *Opduin* (E), 22 Ruyslaan; 02220–17445. 72 rooms with bath. Newly renovated. Pool, sauna, solarium, etc. *Het Gouden Boltje* (M), 44 Dorpstraat; 02220–17755. 15 rooms, closed Nov.-March. *Beatrix* (I), 5 Kamerstraat; 02220–17207. 18 rooms.

Restaurants. *Taverne* (M), 296 Dorpstraat; 02220–17585. Sole is their specialty. *De Buteriggelt* (M–I), 13 Badweg; 02228–17362. Tourist menu.

At **Den Burg,** the island's capital: *den Burg* (I), 2 Emmalaan; 02220–12106. 18 rooms. *De Lindeboom* (M), 14 Groeneplaats; 02220–2041. On the main square.

Restaurants. *Vierspan* (M), 3 Gravenstraat 02220–13176. Traditional French kitchen. *De Raadskelder* (I), 6 Vismarkt; 02220–12235. Menu based on Texel lamb and other foods produced on the island.

Velsen (18 northwest). **Restaurant.** *Taveerne Beeckestijn,* 136 Rijksweg; 02550–14469. Classical French cuisine on the grounds of Huis Beekestijn, an 18th-century mansion with period rooms. Lunch and dinner.

Volendam (14 northeast). *Spaander* (M), 15 Haven; 02993–63595. 80 rooms; good Nederlands Dis restaurant serves regional dishes. *Van Diepen* (M), 38 Haven; 02993–63705. 18 rooms; good restaurant.

Restaurant. *Van den Hogen* (I), 106 Haven; 02993–63775. Tourist menu.

Wijk aan Zee (17 northwest). Quiet seaside resort. *Mare Sanat* (M), 8 Rijckert Aertsweg, 02517–4364. Small, cozy place, with views of the dunes. *De Klughte* (I), 2 Van Ogtropweg; 02517–4304. 20 rooms; breakfast only. *De Wijk* (I), 12 van Ogeropweg; 02517–4350. 15 rooms and good restaurant.

Restaurant. *Sonnevanck* (M), 2 Rijckert Aertsweg.

Zaanse Schans. *De Saense Schans* (I), 32 Lagedijk, Zaandijk; 075–219119. A modern hotel with superb views.

Restaurant. *De Hoop op D'Swarte Walvis* (E), 13–15 Kalverringdijk, Zaandijk; 075–165540/165269. First class French food in idyllic 17th-century maritime setting. Recommended. *De Kraai* (I), 1 Kraaienpad; 075–156403. Tasty pancakes in former 17th-century granary.

Zandvoort aan Zee (18 west). Popular North Sea resort. *Hoogland* (M), 5 Westerparkstraat; 02507–15541. 25 rooms. 5 minutes from golf course. *Esplanade* (I), 2 Badhuisplein; 02507–12073. 30 rooms.

Restaurants. *Freddy en Paul* (M), la Strandpaviljoen; 02507–16959. Right by the beach, international cuisine. *Le Pierrot* (M), 52 Houtestraat, 02507–17822. French food and atmosphere. *De Uitzichttoren* (M), 7 Thorbeckestraat; 02507–12474. In the top of the 200-ft. tower that dominates the town; offers a remarkable view even if the food is so-so. Open 11 A.M.– 10 P.M.

GETTING AROUND. By Car. This is the best way of all for seeing this part of Holland. Distances are short, there are no big cities outside of Haarlem and Hilversum, and you can return to Amsterdam for the night after each excursion, if you wish. You can also stay in smaller, cheaper hotels away from the capital, where parking is also much easier. Buy a good map which will enable you to leave main roads and explore the delightful byways of the region in complete confidence that you can always find your way back at the end of the day by the most direct route. Almost every corner of this country is a delight. Even the remote lanes are paved, so avoid the motorways whenever you can. Dutch roads in the Amsterdam-Rotterdam-Hague region are designed to keep through traffic on the highway. Side roads will cost extra time, but you may see more en route.

A point to remember, whatever your means of transportation, is that nearly every city and town mentioned in this chapter can be visited from Den Haag with almost as much ease as Amsterdam, thanks to the compact nature of this angle of the Netherlands. You might consider, therefore, visiting everything north of Amsterdam (excursions 1 and 2: see text) from that city and then doing the rest from Den Haag or Utrecht, so as to have a little variety.

By Train. All the key towns in this area can be reached very easily by train. On Friday mornings in July and August there are special trains, the Kaasmark (Cheesemarket) Expresses, which leave the Central Station in Amsterdam at 9.03 and 9.32, arriving in Alkmaar in good time for the market; journey takes 30 minutes. Haarlem is also easily reached by trains that leave the Central Station roughly every half hour.

Excursions. A wide variety of inclusive sightseeing tours from Amsterdam are available. Among the many on offer are: a 4-hour bus and boat tour covering Monnickendam, Marken and Volendam, cost is around Fl. 40; an 8-hour tour around the Zuiderzee covering Urk, Hindeloopen, Makkum and Hoorn, cost is around Fl. 70; and Fl. 20 for a 6-hour tour of the Zaanse Schans by boat and bus. For boat trips beginning in Alkmaar, contact Rederij Woltheus; 072–114840. Most of these tours operate between June and September and are by bus starting from the area around the Central Station in Amsterdam. There are also special day excursions organized by the national railway. Ask for details of the NS *Dagtochten* which are excellent value for money. Details of rail tours are available from any NS (Dutch rail) station (*binnenland* window). Information on other tours are available from the VVV in front of the Central Station.

There is also an interesting boat excursion from Harderwijk, which leaves every hour during the summer and lasts about 70 minutes. The trip covers Veluwemeer and the polder reclamation work in progress.

TOURIST INFORMATION. There are regional VVV offices at the following places: **Aalsmeer,** 1 Drie Kolommenplein (tel. 02977–25374); **Alkmaar,** 2 Waagplein (tel. 072–114284); **Bussum,** 6 Wilhelminaplantsoen (tel.035–211651); **Haarlem,** 1 Stationsplein (tel. 023–319059); **Den Helder,** 30 Julianaplein (tel. 02230–25544); **Hilversum,** 2 Emmastraat (tel. 035–211651); **Hoorn,** 21 Nieuwstraat (tel. 02290–18342); **Texel,** 9 Groeneplaats, Den Burg (tel. 02220–14741); **Zaandam,** 76 Gedempte Gracht (tel. 075–162221).

MUSEUMS AND PLACES OF INTEREST. Among the many local museums that deal with the history of various towns in this region, there are a number of more than passing interest to the visitor from abroad.

Aalsmeer. Historische Tuin, 32 Uiterweg. These so-called Historical Gardens represent an open-air museum showing the development of market gardening in the area. Open May–Oct., Mon.–Fri. 10–1, except Wed. 1.30–4; Sat. and Sun. 1.30–4.

Alkmaar. Stadhuis. The Town Hall is open on weekdays 9–12. **Stedelijk Museum** (Municipal Museum), in the House of National Guard. Details facets of the town's development, especially the siege of the Spanish in 1573, which was successfully resisted. Open Tues.–Fri. 10–5, Sun. 1–5. Closed Sat. and Mon. Adm. Fl. 3.

Het Hollands Kaasmuseum, Waaggebouw. Cheesemaking, ancient and modern. Open Apr.–Oct., Mon.–Sat. 10–4. Closed Sun. Fri. 9–4. Adm Fl. 2.

Beermuseum de Boom, 1 Houttil. Open Tues. to Sat. 10–4, Sun. 1–5. Closed Mon. Showing history and old methods of brewing—includes a tasting room! Adm. F1. 2. After your visit, try one of the 86 beers on offer in the bar below the museum.

Bergen. Het Sterkenhuis, 21 Oude Prinseweg. Small museum in house dating from 1655. Has interesting exhibits on the defeat, at Bergen, in 1799 of the Duke of York's British and Russian army by the French. Open May–Sept., Tues.–Sat. 10–12, 3–5. Adm. Fl. 2.

Edam. Edam's Museum, Damplein (opposite Town Hall). Fascinating museum showing how a retired sea captain lived in the 18th century. Richly furnished with period items. Open Easter to Sept. Mon. to Sat. 10–4.30, Sun. 2–4.30.

Kaaswag (Cheese Weight House). In a building dating from 1823; interesting exhibitions on cheese. Open April to end Sept. only, daily 10–5.

Late Gothic House on Damplein with a floating cellar houses the local museum. Open Easter–Sept., Mon.–Sat. 10–4, Sun. 1.30–4.30.

Enkhuizen. Stedelijk Waagmuseum, 8 Kaasmarkt. Open Tue.–Sat. 10–12, 2–5; Sun. 2–5. Located in the old weight house; also, interesting exhibitions of contemporary art in the attic.

Wapenmuseum, located in the old prison; good collections of arms and armor through the ages.

Zuiderzee Buitenmuseum. Open-air museum, opened in 1983; attractive and carefully-reconstructed old buildings, including a church, from around the Zuiderzee. Open Apr.–mid-Oct., daily 10–5. Adm. Fl. 9. (Entrance fee includes *Binnenmuseum.*) Allow about three hours for the open-air museum before you get to the Binnenmuseum, near the Buitenmuseum exit.

Zuiderzee Binnenmuseum, in the Peperhuis. Located in what was once a warehouse belonging to the East India Company, the museum has just been completely refurbished and has good exhibits on many aspects of life in Zuiderzee; fishing, costumes and furniture etc. Open mid-Apr.–mid-Oct., Mon.–Sat. 10–5, Sun. 12–5.

Haarlem. Frans Halsmuseum. 62 Groot Heligland. In early 17th-century almshouse, contains a marvelous collection of pictures by Hals, plus some by contemporaries. Open Mon.–Sat. 11–5, Sun. 1–5. Adm. Fl. 5.

Teylers Museum, 16 Spaarne. The oldest museum in the country, it claims, established by wealthy merchant in 1778 as museum of science and arts. Has a number of drawings by Michelangelo and Raphael. Open Tues.–Sat. 10–5, Sun. 1–5 (closes one hour earlier in winter). Closed Mon. Adm. Fl. 3.50.

De Hallen, Grote Markt. Changing exhibitions of ancient and modern art, town history, sculpture and tapestries. Open Mon.–Sat. 11–5, Sun. 1–5.

St. Bavo Basilica. Open Apr.–Sept., Mon.–Sat. 10–12, 2–4.30, Sun. 2–4.30. (Not to be confused with the Grote Kerk, which is also dedicated to St. Bavo.)

Corrie ten Boomhuis Museum, 19 Barteljorisstraat, (near the Grote Markt); 023–310324. This watchmaker's house and shop, filmed for TV as "The Hiding Place," gave refuge to those fleeing from Nazi persecution. Open Apr.–Oct., Mon.–Sat. 10–4.30; other months, 11–3.30; Closed Sun.

Haarlemmermeer. Museum de Cruquius, 32 Cruquiusdijk. Housed in historic polder pumping station built in 1849, museum provides excellent coverage of the country's battle against the sea and the draining of polders. Good models of windmills etc. Open Apr.–Sept. Mon.–Sat. 10–5, Sun. 12–5. Oct.–Nov. Mon.–Sat. 10–4, Sun. 12–4. Adm. Fl. 4.

Den Helder. Helders Marinemuseum (Maritime Museum), 3 Hoofdgracht. Located in attractive building dating from 1820s; traces the history of the Dutch Royal Navy since 1813. Open Jan. to Nov., Tues.–Fri. 10–5, Sat. and Sun. 1–4.30. During Summer, also open Mon. 1–5. Adm. Fl. 3.

Wadlopen (Mud-walking) to Texel island. For information and reservations, contact the NBT or the Pieterburen Foundation, 118 Hoofstraat, Pieterburen; 05952–345. You can always walk one way and take the ferry back!

Hoorn. Westfries Museum, 1 Rode Steen. Located in beautiful building dating from 1632; museum traces the development of the town, especially the exploration and colonization of the Far East in which Hoorn played a leading role. Open Mon.–Fri. 11–5, Sat. and Sun. 2–5. Adm. Fl. 3.50.

Stoomtram Hoorn, Medemblik. A delightful old steam train runs for 20 km from Hoorn to Medemblik. Trains run daily in July and Aug., and Tues.–Sat. in May, June, and Sept. and connect with a boat trip from Medemblik to Enkhuizen. (Tel. 02290–14862.) Open May to Sept. From Enkhuizen you can return to Hoorn by regular train (Fl. 30 round trip) or take a day trip, which includes the steam train, the boat trip, and regular train fare, available from any Dutch train station.

Koog aan der Zaan. Molenmuseum (Windmill Museum). 18 Museumlaan. History of the windmill in Holland; models, pictures, etc. Open Mon.–Fri. 10–5, Sat. and Sun. 2–5. Adm. Fl. 3.50.

Laren. Singer Museum, 1 Oude Drift. Works of William Henry Singer Jr.; paintings of the American, French and Dutch schools, changing exhibitions. Open Tues. to Sat. 11–5, Sun. 12–5. Adm. Fl. 5.

Lelystad. Informatiecentrum Nieuwland. Oostvaardersdijk 1–13. History of the draining and reclamation of the IJsselmeer and the building of the town of Lelystad; tel. 03200–60799. Open daily 10–5. In the boatyard next door is a replica of the *Batavia,* a Dutch East India clipper ship under construction. Open daily 9–5. To appreciate the immensity of this land reclamation, try a dramatic sightseeing flight over the region (*Martinair,* Emoeweg Airport; 03202–476, or *Wings Over Holland;* 03200–260).

Lisse. Museum voor de Bloembollenstreek, 219 Heereweg. History and culture of bulbs and local area. Open Apr.–May, Tues.–Sun. 10–5; June–Mar., Tues.–Fri. 1–5, Sat. and Sun. 12.30–5.

Limmen. Hortus Bulborum Museum, 64 Dusseldorperweg. Outdoor museum with living history of bulb cultivation, including some original stock. Open mid-Apr.–mid-May, Mon.–Thurs. 9–noon, 2–4; Fri. 9–noon.

Marken. Marker Museum, 44–47 Kerkburt. This museum is built from four "smoke-houses," typical fishing cottages designed with a hole in the roof to allow the smoke to escape. Open Easter–Nov. Mon.–Sat. 10–4.30, Sun 2–5; Dec.–Good Fri. daily 2–5. Adm. Fl. 5.

Medemblik. Radboud Castle. Open mid-May–mid-Sept. Mon.–Sat. 10–5, Sun. 2–5; late Sept.–early May, Sun. only 2–5. Adm. Fl. 5.

Muiden. Muiderslot. 13th-century moated castle; fascinating both inside and out. A tavern in the wine cellar is open from April to the end of August. Open Apr.–Sept., Mon.–Fri. 10–5, Sun. 1–5. Oct.–Mar., Mon.–Fri. 10–3, Sun. 1–3. Adm. F. 4.50.

Naarden. Vesting Museum (Fortification Museum), 6 Westwalstraat. Underground and open-air museum with casemates, cannon-cellar and collection of historical objects. Open Apr.–mid-Oct., Mon.–Fri. 10–4.30, Sat. and Sun. 12–5. Adm. Fl. 4.

Sneek. Stadhuis. The Town Hall is open daily 10–12, 1.30–5.

Texel. Nature Recreation Center, 92 Ruyslaan, De Koog. This key spot houses the public aquarium plus the seal and bird hospital. The seals eat at 3.30 P.M. Reservations for bird-watching can be made here as well (02220–17741). Open Apr. through Oct. Mon.–Sat. 9–5. Adm. Fl. 5. You can also take a guided tour of the Slufter nature reserve, Apr.–Aug. at 8 A.M., or possibly visit the Muy and Geul reserves Apr.–Aug. from 11 A.M. For any of these excursions, boots are essential equipment!

Marinemuseum, 21 Barendszstraat, Oudeschild. Situated in a former corn and seaweed barn; contains a fascinating collection of beachcomber discoveries, plus an exhibition of the Russian War. Open Apr.–end Oct., Tues.–Sat. 9–5.

Zaandam. De Zaanse Schans, Kalverringdijk. Open-air collection of typical old wooden buildings, windmills, houses and shops, all furnished. Open daily, year-round; telephone 075–162221 for more information.

SHOPPING. Cheese is the great specialty throughout this area. It's best bought at the various colorful markets that most towns hold. Usually the vendors will let you sample their wares. All the most popular places also have shops selling the full range of the country's crafts industry. For bulb lovers, Lisse is the place to head for. Special arrangements can be made for sending bulbs home (direct importation is not generally allowed).

Moving upmarket, Haarlem is renowned for its antique shops, with prices generally lower than in Amsterdam or Den Haag.

CRUISES. For 50-minute waterborne trips around the windmill region, contact Rederij de Schans; 075–172920.

ENGLISH-DUTCH VOCABULARY

USEFUL EXPRESSIONS

English	Dutch
Please	Alstublieft
Thank you very much	Dank U zeer
Good morning, sir	Dag, Mijnheer
Good evening, madam	Goedenavond, Mevrouw
Good night	Goedenacht
Goodbye	Tot ziens
Excuse me	Pardón
Hunger, thirst	Honger, dorst
I am hungry, thirsty	Ik heb honger, dorst
Yes, no	Ja, nee
Yesterday, today, tomorrow	Gisteren, vandaag, morgen
This evening, this morning	Vanavond, vanmorgen
How much?	Hoeveel?
Expensive, cheap	Duur, goedkoop
Where? Where is? Where are?	Waar? Waar is? Waar zijn?
Is this the right way to . . . ?	Is dit de goede weg naar . . . ?
Can you direct me to the	Kunt u mij . . . dichtsbijzijnde . . .
nearest . . . ?	wijzen?
doctor	de . . . dokter
hotel/restaurant	het . . . hotel/restaurant
garage	de . . . garage
post office	het . . . postkantoor
police station	het . . . politiebureau
telephone	de . . . telefoon
Left, right	Links, rechts
To the left/right	Naar links/rechts
Bus/trolley stop	Bus/tram halte
Entrance	Ingang
Exit	Uitgang
Admission free	Vrije toegang
Open from . . . to . . .	Geopend van . . . tot . . .
No smoking	Verboden te roken
Gentlemen	Heren
Ladies	Dames

RESTAURANTS AND DINING

Please give us the menu	Mag ik het menu
What do you recommend?	Wat kunt U aanbevelen?

Please give us the table d'hôte	Wij nemen table d'hôte
Please serve us as quickly as possible	Bedien ons zo vlug mogelijk, alstublieft
Please give me the check (bill)	Ober, kan ik betalen?
Have you included the tip?	Is dit inclusief fooi?
Waiter! Waitress!	Ober! Juffrouw!
Please give us some . . .	Geeft u ons wat . . .
Bread and butter	Brood en boter
Toast	Geroostered brood
buttered	warm gesmeerd
dry	zonder boter
Jam	Jam
Marmalade	Marmelade
Cheese	Kaas
Sugar	Suiker
Salt	Zout
Pepper	Peper
Mustard	Mosterd

Drinks

Water	Water
Iced water	Met ijsblokjes
Mineral water	Mineraalwater
Milk	Melk
Coffee	Koffie
Coffee with hot milk/cream	Koffie verkeerd (koffie met hete melk)/room
Tea, iced tea	Thee, thé glacé
Hot chocolate	Warme chocolademelk
Beer	Bier
Wine (red, white)	Wijn (rode, witte)
A bottle of . . .	Een fles . . .
A pot of . . .	Een potje . . .
A glass of . . .	Een glas . . .
A cup of . . .	Een kop . . .

AT THE HOTEL

Can you recommend a good hotel?	Kunt u me een goed hotel aanraden?
Which is the best hotel?	Wat is het beste hotel?
Have you anything cheaper?	Hebt u iets goedkoper?
What is the price including breakfast?	Wat is de prijs inclusief ontbijt?
Does the price include service?	Geldt de prijs inclusief bediening?
At what time is . . .	Hoe laat is . . .
breakfast?	het ontbijt?
lunch?	het middageten?
dinner?	het avondeten?
Please wake me at . . . o'clock	Ik wil graag om . . . uur gewekt worden
I want this dry-cleaned	Kunt U dit laten stomen?

I want these clothes washed	Wilt U alstublieft deze kleren laten wassen
I would like to have a . . .	Ik zou . . . willen hebben
single room	een eenpersoonskamer
double room with	een kamer met
twin beds	twee bedden
double bed	een tweepersoonsbed
with bath	met bad
Another pillow	Nog een kussen
Another blanket	Nog een deken
Soap, towel	Zeep, handdoek

TRAVELING BY TRAIN

Timetable	Dienstregeling
Through train	Doorgaande trein
Slow train	Stoptrein
Fast train	Sneltrein/Intercity
Express train	Exprestrein
Weekdays only	Op werkdagen
Sundays and holidays only	Op zon- en feestdagen
Return ticket	Retour
One-way ticket	Enkele reis
Fare	Prijs van het kaartje
Compartment	Coupé
Dining car	Restauratiewagen
Sleeping compartment	Slaapcoupé
First class	Eerste klas
Second class	Tweede klas
Delay	Vertraging
Connection	Aansluiting
All aboard	Instappen

AT THE POST OFFICE

Air mail	Luchtpost
Ordinary mail	Gewone post
Special delivery	Expresse
Cable	Telegram
Stamp	Postzegel
Registered	Aangetekend

MOTORING

How many kilometers is it to . . . ?	Hoeveel kilometers is het naar . . . ?
I want . . . liters of gasoline	Ik wens . . . liter benzine
Fill it up, please	Bijvullen, alstublieft
Will you . . .	Wilt U . . .
grease the car	de wagen doorsmeren
change the oil	de olie vernieuwen
check the oil	de olie controleren

wash the car	de wagen wassen
clean the windscreen (windshield)	de voorruit schoonmaken
top up the battery with distilled water	de accu met gedistilleerd water bijvullen
What will it cost?	Hoeveel kost dat?
May I park here?	Mag ik hier parkeren?
Sound your horn	Claxoneren, signaal geven
Slow	Langzaam
To the right	Rechtsaf
To the left	Linksaf
Crossroads	Kruispunt
No admission	Verboden toegang
Keep to your right	Rechts houden
Level crossing	Spoorwegkruising
Road up for repair	Opgebroken rijweg
Road blocked	Geen doorgaand verkeer
No traffic allowed	Verboden voor alle verkeer
One-way street	Eénrichtingsverkeer
Traffic lights	Verkeerslichten
Straight ahead	Rechtdoor
Maximum speed	Maximum snelheid

DAYS OF THE WEEK

Monday	maandag
Tuesday	dinsdag
Wednesday	woensdag
Thursday	donderdag
Friday	vrijdag
Saturday	zaterdag
Sunday	zondag

NUMERALS

one	een (ayn)
two	twee (tvay)
three	drie (dree)
four	vier (feer)
five	vijf (fife)
six	zes (sess)
seven	zeven (zayfern)
eight	acht (ahgt)
nine	negen (nayghen)
ten	tien (teen)
eleven	elf (elf)
twelve	twaalf (tvahlf)
thirteen	dertien (derrteen)
fourteen	veertien (fairteen)
fifteen	vijftien (fifeteen)
sixteen	zestien (zessteen)
seventeen	zeventien (zayfenteen)

eighteen	achttien (ahgteen)
nineteen	negentien (nayhgenteen)
twenty	twintig (tvintuhk)
twenty-one	een en twintig (ayn en tvintuhk)
twenty-two	twee en twintig (tvay en tvintuhk)
thirty	dertig (derrtuhk)
forty	veeertig (fairtuhk)
fifty	vijftig (fifetuhk)
sixty	zestig (zesstuhk)
seventy	zeventig (zayfentuhk)
eighty	tachtig (tahktuhk)
ninety	negentig (naygentuhk)
one hundred	honderd (hondert)
one hundred and ten	honderd tien (hondert teen)
two hundred	tweehonderd (tvay hondert)
one thousand	duizend (doyzent)

Index

The letter H indicates hotels and other accommodations.
The letter R indicates restaurants.

Fodor's Travel Guides

U.S. Guides

Alaska
Arizona
Boston
California
Cape Cod, Martha's
  Vineyard, Nantucket
The Carolinas & the
  Georgia Coast
The Chesapeake
  Region
Chicago
Colorado
Disney World & the
  Orlando Area
Florida
Hawaii

Las Vegas, Reno,
  Tahoe
Los Angeles
Maine, Vermont,
  New Hampshire
Maui
Miami & the
  Keys
National Parks
  of the West
New England
New Mexico
New Orleans
New York City
New York City
  (Pocket Guide)

Pacific North Coast
Philadelphia & the
  Pennsylvania
  Dutch Country
Puerto Rico
  (Pocket Guide)
The Rockies
San Diego
San Francisco
San Francisco
  (Pocket Guide)
The South
Santa Fe, Taos,
  Albuquerque
Seattle &
  Vancouver

Texas
USA
The U. S. & British
  Virgin Islands
The Upper Great
  Lakes Region
Vacations in
  New York State
Vacations on the
  Jersey Shore
Virginia & Maryland
Waikiki
Washington, D.C.
Washington, D.C.
  (Pocket Guide)

Foreign Guides

Acapulco
Amsterdam
Australia
Austria
The Bahamas
The Bahamas
  (Pocket Guide)
Baja & Mexico's Pacific
  Coast Resorts
Barbados
Barcelona, Madrid,
  Seville
Belgium &
  Luxembourg
Berlin
Bermuda
Brazil
Budapest
Budget Europe
Canada
Canada's Atlantic
  Provinces

Cancun, Cozumel,
  Yucatan Peninsula
Caribbean
Central America
China
Czechoslovakia
Eastern Europe
Egypt
Europe
Europe's Great Cities
France
Germany
Great Britain
Greece
The Himalayan
  Countries
Holland
Hong Kong
India
Ireland
Israel
Italy

Italy 's Great Cities
Jamaica
Japan
Kenya, Tanzania,
  Seychelles
Korea
London
London
  (Pocket Guide)
London Companion
Mexico
Mexico City
Montreal &
  Quebec City
Morocco
New Zealand
Norway
Nova Scotia,
  New Brunswick,
  Prince Edward
  Island
Paris

Paris (Pocket Guide)
Portugal
Rome
Scandinavia
Scandinavian Cities
Scotland
Singapore
South America
South Pacific
Southeast Asia
Soviet Union
Spain
Sweden
Switzerland
Sydney
Thailand
Tokyo
Toronto
Turkey
Vienna & the Danube
  Valley
Yugoslavia

Wall Street Journal Guides to Business Travel

Europe   International Cities   Pacific Rim   USA & Canada

Special-Interest Guides

Bed & Breakfast and
  Country Inn Guides:
  Mid-Atlantic Region
New England
The South
The West

Cruises and Ports
  of Call
Healthy Escapes
Fodor's Flashmaps
  New York

Fodor's Flashmaps
  Washington, D.C.
Shopping in Europe
Skiing in the USA &
  Canada

Smart Shopper's
  Guide to London
Sunday in New York
Touring Europe
Touring USA